# Dessert Cooking for Two

# dessert COOKING for two

### 115 *Perfectly Portioned* Sweets for Every Occasion

**Robin Donovan**

Photography by Evi Abeler

**R**

ROCKRIDGE
PRESS

Interior and Cover Designer: Darren Samuel
Photo Art Director: Sue Smith
Editor: Rachel Feldman
Production Editor: Erum Khan

Photography © 2019 Evi Abeler. Food styling by Albane Sharrard.

Cover: Classic Ice Cream Sandwiches, page 180

ISBN: Print 978-1-64152-571-8 | eBook 978-1-64152-572-5

*To my husband, Doug,*
*for always sharing his sweets,*
*and this sweet life, with me.*

# Contents

Introduction viii

## Part One
## *Dessert-Making For Duos*

**1** MAKING TWO EASY
2

**2** DESSERT TECHNIQUES AND SKILLS
12

## Part Two
## *Recipes*

**3** COOKIES, BROWNIES, AND BARS
22

**4** CUPCAKES AND CAKES
52

**5** PIES, TARTS, AND CRUMBLES
86

**6** PASTRIES AND CONFECTIONS
120

**7** PUDDINGS, CUSTARDS, AND CRÈMES
142

**8** FROZEN TREATS
164

Measurement Conversions 186

Fruity, Chocolatey, or Creamy? 187

Just Egg White, Just Egg Yolk, Small Amount of Flour? 189

General Index 190

# *Introduction*

I grew up in the original health-food mecca—Berkeley, California—in the 1970s. My parents were determined to raise their kids on unprocessed foods with as little refined sugar as possible. Instead of fluffy white bread, we got dense, dry slabs studded with rock-hard bits of whole grains and sprouted seeds. Instead of cookies, we got gritty whole-wheat, honey-sweetened fig bars from the bulk bins at the local co-op. Our parents even tried to convince us that carob was a reasonable substitute for chocolate (they were lying).

As a general rule, my mother banished junk food from our home, which only made me more determined to feed my cravings for sweet, unnaturally colored, and decidedly not nutritious foods. Every penny of my allowance went straight to the closest candy store, and you can bet I made fast friends with the few neighborhood kids whose parents hadn't jumped on the health-food bandwagon.

One thing my health-conscious mother did have a weakness for, however, was chocolate. She didn't bake big chocolate cakes, dozens of double chocolate cookies, or sinfully rich chocolate cream pies, but she did keep a bag of Hershey's miniature chocolate bars in the pantry at all times. My mother would have a single mini chocolate bar after dinner. She had a sweet tooth, but she was a master of moderation. Those mini bars were perfect because they came with built-in portion control, unlike a layer cake or a full-size batch of cookies. As a child, I, of course, regarded this as pure insanity. As I got older, I mostly defaulted to keeping sweets out of the house to avoid temptation.

It wasn't until I had a child—who was just as drawn to all the sugary stuff as I was—that I really wanted to make delicious, homemade desserts while also emphasizing moderation. I didn't want to make sweets off-limits to my kid because I knew firsthand that would just make him want them more. On the other hand, keeping quantities of desserts around the house proved too tempting for me, my son, and my husband. That's when I started playing around with small-batch baking.

Consciously cooking for two means worrying less about waste and money, trying new recipes at home, and feeling good about indulging in moderation. The best part is that it doesn't matter who you're cooking for or with—a small family, a significant other, a friend, or even just you (some for now and some for later). I hope this book will help you enjoy what you love with those you love.

# How to Use This Book

Small-batch baking is a great way to enjoy homemade desserts while also keeping your indulgences in check. What could be better than baking just six cookies or a pie that's the perfect size for two people? No longer will you have to resist the temptation presented by an endless pan of fudgy brownies or a platter of cookies large enough to feed the whole neighborhood. The recipes here have been tested to ensure the right proportions of each ingredient and utilize some reduction tricks that make it possible to produce the same crave-worthy desserts you love—just in smaller portions.

These recipes cover a range of delicious desserts—from cookies, brownies, and bars to frozen treats and everything in between. To help you navigate this bounty of treats, you'll find the following helpful labels accompanying the recipes:

- **Quick:** Made in 30 minutes or less

- **No-Bake:** Does not require an oven or stovetop

- **Mini Equipment:** Uses special mini equipment, like a 6-inch pie pan

- **Lightly Sweet:** Indicates a lighter option with less sugar

This book offers more than 100 perfectly portioned recipes that cater to every kind of dessert lover, whether you're a fan of American classics, unique flavors, or lighter treats. You'll also find lessons in how to be successful with small-batch dessert making, equipment hacks when you don't have specialized equipment, cooking tips and ideas for ingredient substitutions, and ideas for utilizing leftover ingredients.

*Now you can have your cake*
*and eat it—all of it—too.*

Part One

# Dessert-Making For Duos

# 1
# MAKING TWO EASY

While it's pretty easy to modify savory recipes to make fewer servings, it's a bit more complicated with desserts. Baking, more than any other type of cooking, relies on carefully balanced proportions of liquid and dry ingredients, leaveners, sweeteners, and foundational ingredients like flour. Simply halving or quartering the measurements doesn't always produce the result you want. Additionally, there's the problem of eggs. How do you halve a recipe that calls for one egg, or three? It may not be as simple as just cutting a recipe in half or quarters, but with a few tricks and careful testing, you can make fantastic desserts in small portions.

It all starts with a bit of know-how on shopping for ingredients in small quantities, tricks for cutting hard-to-divide ingredients like eggs, and some clever ideas for cookware.

# Portioning for Two

When making dessert for two, it's not only the ingredient list that matters—the equipment you use is also important. You may be surprised to find that mini equipment even exists (sadly, mini pie dishes have yet to become a household staple). If you find that you're passionate about mini desserts, I encourage you to eventually invest in some of the pieces detailed below, which are very handy when making desserts for two. But the great news is that none of the recipes in this book require you to go out and buy any special mini equipment. For every recipe that calls for mini equipment, you'll also find an "equipment hack" that explains how to make the recipe using a more common baking vessel. We've detailed some examples below.

## MINI EQUIPMENT

*Mini loaf pan:* Loaf pans are baking pans (usually made of metal, but they can be glass or ceramic) that are shaped like a standard loaf of bread you would find at the grocery store. Full-size loaf pans are usually 9-by-5-by-3 inches or 8-by-4-by-3 inches. A mini loaf pan is around 6-by-3-by-2½ inches.

❧ *Equipment hack:* If you don't have a mini loaf pan, you can substitute two 8-ounce ramekins. You may need to shave off a little cooking time, though, so check your desserts a minute or two before the recommended cooking time is up.

*Mini muffin tin:* A mini muffin tin usually has 24 wells or cups that each hold 1½ to 2 ounces of batter.

❧ *Equipment hack:* You can use a regular muffin tin and put your batter into disposable mini muffin or mini cupcake foil liners. Or, if you're working with dough, you can place it directly into the wells of a regular muffin tin and use a shot glass to shape the crust around.

*Mini pie dish:* A 6-inch round glass, ceramic, or metal baking dish with angled sides, designed specifically for baking (mini) pies.

❧ *Equipment hack:* You can use two 8-ounce ramekins or oven-safe, widemouthed canning jar lids and rings to replace one mini pie dish.

*Mini round cake pans:* 6-inch round, square, or rectangular metal baking pans with 2-inch sides.

❧ *Equipment hack:* You can use two 8-ounce ramekins instead. For cakes that can be micro-waved, you can also use microwave-safe coffee mugs.

*Ice pop mold:* Often made of plastic or silicone, an ice pop mold usually has 6 ice-pop-shaped wells and sticks or handles that are inserted before freezing the liquid.

❧ *Equipment hack:* Instead of an ice pop mold, you can use disposable paper cups and wooden ice pop sticks.

## OTHER EQUIPMENT

*Baking sheet (aka cookie sheet):* A flat metal sheet pan with a lip on one or both short sides for gripping. A rimmed baking sheet has a short rim all the way around the edges. Both types are usually made of aluminum or steel.

*Canning jar lids and rings:* The metal lids and rings for canning jars can be used for baking, and they're the perfect size for making mini pies and tartlets. Be sure to place the flat metal lid in the ring with the rubberized side down so that you are cooking on the part that is uncoated metal.

*Electric mixer:* This can be either a handheld electric mixer with two beaters attached or a stand mixer, which is a self-contained electric mixer that stands on the countertop. It has a housing that locks the beater or beaters in place over a mounting base that holds a mixing bowl.

*Food processor:* An electric appliance that mixes and chops ingredients using interchangeable blades.

*Measuring cups and spoons:* You'll need a set of dry measuring cups designed to be filled to the rim with dry ingredients and leveled off (¼, ⅓, ½, and 1 cup), a liquid measuring cup with a spout and increment markings on the side (ideally 2-cup size), and a standard set of measuring spoons (⅛ teaspoon, ¼ teaspoon, ½ teaspoon, 1 teaspoon, and 1 tablespoon).

*Mixing bowls:* A set of three mixing bowls (small, medium, and large) for mixing ingredients. I recommend glass or ceramic mixing bowls because, unlike metal, they are unreactive, meaning they won't react with highly acidic ingredients. The most common acidic ingredients in baking are: applesauce, baking powder, brown sugar, buttermilk, chocolate, cream of tartar, lemon juice, lime juice, molasses, non-Dutch-process (i.e. natural) cocoa powder, sour cream, vinegar, and yogurt.

*Parchment paper:* Similar to wax paper but coated with heat-resistant silicone instead of wax so it can be used in the oven. Like wax paper, parchment paper is both grease-resistant and moisture-resistant. You can find it in the supermarket next to the wax paper and aluminum foil.

*Pastry brush:* Also called a basting brush, this brush is designed for spreading glaze over pastries, cakes, and breads or applying an egg wash over a crust.

*Pastry cutter (or pastry blender):* A tool used to mix fat (such as butter or shortening) into flour when making pastries. Pastry cutters are usually made of narrow strips of metal or wire that are attached to a handle. To use it, place the fat and flour in a mixing bowl and press the metal strips or wire into the fat to cut it into small pieces while blending it with the flour.

*Pie weights:* Small metal, glass, or ceramic balls used to weigh down a piecrust for blind baking (see page 18).

*Ramekin:* An oven-safe glass or ceramic dish, usually round with straight sides, intended to be used as both a baking and serving vessel. Ramekins come in a wide range of sizes, but the most commonly used in recipes are 4-, 6-, or 8-ounce ramekins.

*Rolling pin:* A typical American-style rolling pin is usually made of wood and has a center rod controlled by two handles on the ends that turns inside an outer cylinder. A rolling pin is essential for rolling out dough to an even thickness.

*Rubber spatula:* A flexible, rectangular or rounded rubber (or silicone) head on a long handle used for stirring, folding, spreading ingredients, and scraping mixing bowls.

*Saucepan:* A small, round cooking pot with tall sides. Usually made of metal, it is used on the stovetop.

*Sieve:* Also known as a strainer, this is a utensil used for straining solids from liquids. It consists of a handle or handles attached to a (plastic or metal) mesh bowl.

*Skillet (sauté pan):* A round metal pan with slanted sides and a straight handle that is used on the stovetop for frying, stir-frying, or sautéing.

*Whisk:* A long handle with several metal or wire loops joined to it. A whisk is used to blend ingredients while incorporating air into the mixture (see page 16).

*Wire rack:* Also known as a cooling rack, this is a platform made up of metal rods or wires set in a crisscross pattern. The rack allows air to circulate under and around hot food so it cools quickly. Some wire racks have two or three layers so you can cool a lot of cookies or other baked goods at once.

## Shopping for Two

Making desserts in small quantities keeps you from having lots of leftover sweets around the house tempting you or going to waste. But when you shop it is often difficult or expensive to buy key ingredients in the smaller quantities you need for small-batch baking. Here are a few ways you can keep your costs down and minimize waste.

*Buy pantry staples in larger quantities.* Staples like all-purpose flour and sugar (granulated, powdered, and brown) will last a long time, and large packages are more cost-effective than small packages. There is one caveat, though: If you have access to a grocery store that sells these items in bulk bins, you can both save money and get just what you need when you need it.

*Store items properly.* Brown sugar can be a tricky ingredient to store. When the moisture in brown sugar evaporates, the sugar can turn into a rock-hard lump. The simplest way to prevent this is to store the sugar in an airtight container—anything from a fancy jar with a tight seal to a resealable plastic bag with any excess air squeezed out of it.

*Buy produce loose whenever possible.* Some stores sell fruits in bags or other packaging so that you're forced to buy six apples when you only need two. If it is a fruit you'll likely eat on its own or use in other recipes, great, but if not, find a store that allows you to buy fruits individually and get just what you need.

*Except when buying frozen goods.* Many fruits freeze surprisingly well, so you can buy a large package of frozen berries, peaches, pineapple, and other fruits and keep them in the freezer for months. If you have more fresh fruit than you can use, freeze it instead of letting it go to waste.

*Don't buy perishable ingredients in bulk.* Don't make the mistake of trying to save money by buying larger packages of eggs, sour cream, cream cheese, etc., if you know you don't have other uses for them. If you need 2 ounces of sour cream, buy the smallest possible container, unless sour cream is an ingredient you use often. It doesn't save money if you end up throwing most of the container away.

*Do buy butter in bulk.* Butter is often cheaper purchased by the pound, or it can be purchased when it's on sale. The great thing about butter is that it will last forever in the freezer, so go ahead and buy the whole pound when you only need one 4-ounce stick. Keep in mind that the recipes in this book use only unsalted butter.

*Look for ingredients in single-serve containers.* Some ingredients, like yogurt, applesauce, juices, and milk, are commonly sold this way.

## Pantry Staples for Dessert

Whether you're baking giant sheet cakes or a single mug cake, there are certain ingredients that you'll always want to stock in your pantry. While individual recipes will call for ingredients specific to those recipes, these are the staples that appear repeatedly throughout the book.

- All-purpose flour: The recipes in this book can be made with all-purpose flour, so there's no need to stock pastry, cake, bread, or other types of flour.

- Sugar: granulated, confectioners' (powdered), brown

- Eggs: whole, whites, yolks (these recipes have been tested using large eggs)

- Butter: unsalted

- Milk: low-fat or whole (these are interchangeable unless a recipe specifies one or the other)

- Heavy (whipping) cream

- Pure vanilla extract

- Salt: Any basic, fine-grained salt will do, whether it is a table salt, which has iodine added, additive-free kosher salt, or additive-free, mineral-rich sea salt.

- Baking spray: Nonstick cooking spray with flour added, to prevent baked goods from sticking to the pan.

## Making Use of Leftover Ingredients

No matter how carefully you shop, you're bound to end up with some excess ingredients when you're making desserts for two. With that in mind, there's an index at the end of the book that lists recipes to use if you only have one egg yolk, one egg white, or only have a small amount of flour left (page 189). Below are some general tips for what to do if you don't want to use leftovers in a different recipe.

### LEFTOVER DAIRY PRODUCTS

Extra milk is great over cereal or drinking it straight (with a few cookies, perhaps?). Cream can be lightly sweetened and whipped, making it a perfect topping for a host of desserts or even just a bowl full of fresh berries. Sweetened condensed milk is a dreamy substitute for both sugar and cream or milk in your coffee or tea. There are also numerous recipes in the book that use small quantities of it, including Caramel Crumb Bars (page 48), No-Bake Key Lime Pie Cups (page 105), White Chocolate and Toasted Almond Fudge (page 137), and Easy No-Churn Vanilla Ice Cream (page 166). To store leftover sweetened condensed milk, transfer it from the can to an airtight container and refrigerate for up to 2 weeks.

Butter can be frozen indefinitely. Cream cheese can be spread on a bagel or stirred into a pasta sauce for added richness.

### LEFTOVER EGGS

Whole eggs can be turned into omelets or scrambles or hard-boiled for a quick snack. But when a recipe calls for just whites or yolks, what are you supposed to do with what's left?

Egg whites can be refrigerated in an airtight container for up to three days, but they'll keep much longer in the freezer. I put each egg white into one well of an ice cube tray and freeze them that way. Once frozen, you can transfer the cubes to a freezer-safe resealable plastic bag. They can be defrosted in a bowl at room temperature and used in any recipe that calls for egg whites, such as Spicy Ginger Cookies (page 28), Coconut Almond Chocolate Chunk Cookies (page 31), Mocha Meringue Kisses (page 37), or Lemon Pudding Cakes (page 85).

Egg yolks don't freeze as well as whites, but they will last in the refrigerator for a few days. Refrigerate them either whole and covered with a bit of water, or break the yolks and whisk in a bit of water. They'll last in the refrigerator for up to three days. Yolks only are used in lots of recipes for cookies, brownies, cakes, cheesecakes, pie fillings, and custards, including The Very Best Chocolate Chip Cookies (page 24), Double Chocolate Cookies (page 29), Butterscotch Blondies (page 38), Coffee and Cream Brownies (page 40), Blueberry Cheesecake Bars (page 47), Banana Cream Mini Pies (page 92), and Mixed Berry and Pastry Cream Tartlet (page 112).

## LEFTOVER FLOUR

Refined wheat flour has a long shelf life and will last for up to two years if stored in a cool, dry place. If you end up with a small amount and you just want to use it up, a few tablespoons stirred into a stew or sauce is great for thickening. Remember that when making pastries, pie, or tart crusts, or any cookie that is rolled and cut out before baking, you'll need a bit of flour to dust the work surface and rolling pin to prevent the dough from sticking.

# The Deal with Storage

The recipes in this book are designed to make enough for two people. But, of course, everyone eats different amounts, and you may find that you end up with small amounts of leftovers anyway. Or you may want to make dessert ahead of time. Following are tips for storing different types of desserts.

***Cakes, cupcakes, and muffins without frosting:*** These can be stored on a plate or platter, covered tightly with plastic wrap, at room temperature up to 5 days or frozen for up to 3 months. If frozen, thaw in the refrigerator overnight before serving or adding frosting.

***Cakes and cupcakes with frosting:*** The frosting forms a seal over the cake, preventing it from drying out, so you don't need to cover these tightly with plastic wrap. Store these lightly covered at room temperature for up to 5 days. An exception to this is cake that has been sliced—be sure to cover the cut sides with plastic wrap to prevent drying.

***Cookies:*** Soft cookies should be stored in an airtight container at room temperature for up to 5 days. Store crisp cookies loosely covered at room temperature for up to 5 days. Cookies can be stored in the freezer, in resealable plastic bags, for up to 3 months.

**Brownies and bars:** Leave brownies and bars in the baking pan uncut and tightly wrapped with plastic wrap. Alternatively, remove the whole thing from the pan (still uncut) and wrap tightly in plastic wrap. Once cut, store in an airtight container separated by pieces of parchment paper. They'll stay fresh for up to 3 days. You can also freeze for up to 3 months.

**Pies and tarts:** Cover fruit pies with plastic wrap and store at room temperature for up to 2 days or in the refrigerator for 3 to 5 days. Uncut fruit pies can be frozen, tightly wrapped with plastic wrap, for up to 3 months. Unbaked fruit pies can be frozen for up to 3 months and then baked without thawing. Pies with egg-based fillings like pumpkin, custard, and cream pies should be stored, covered with plastic wrap, in the refrigerator for up to 4 days.

# 2
# DESSERT TECHNIQUES AND SKILLS

Making desserts calls on many cooking techniques common to preparing savory recipes, but other techniques are unique to preparing sweets. If you are an experienced baker, many of these techniques may already be familiar to you. If you are new to making desserts, the information in this chapter will help you better understand the instructions in the dessert recipes.

# Melting Chocolate

In making desserts, chocolate is sometimes added as chunks, chips, or powder. But often chocolate must be melted first. Chocolate is a delicate substance and must be handled correctly. Put it in a saucepan over direct heat (as you might melt butter), and there's a good chance it will burn or turn grainy. Here are the three best ways to melt chocolate.

## MELTING CHOCOLATE IN A MICROWAVE

Using a microwave is the easiest, and perhaps most foolproof, way to melt chocolate. Here's how: Break or chop the chocolate into small pieces (unless you are using chips or wafers) and place in a microwave-safe bowl. Heat in the microwave on 50 percent power (or whatever is the lowest setting on your microwave) for 30 to 60 seconds. The chocolate should be partially melted. Stir the chocolate until it is completely melted and smooth. If the first stint in the microwave doesn't melt the chocolate enough, put it back in and heat, again on 50 percent power, for another 30 seconds. Stir until completely melted and smooth.

## MELTING CHOCOLATE IN A DOUBLE BOILER

A double boiler is another simple and fail-safe way to melt chocolate. A true double boiler is a pair of stacking saucepans. The lower saucepan holds boiling water. The top saucepan holds the chocolate, which is melted by the gentle heat of the steam from the boiling water. You can hack your own double boiler with a heat-safe mixing bowl (stainless steel is the best) and a saucepan with water in it.

Whichever equipment setup you choose, fill the bottom pan with about 1 inch of water and bring to a simmer. Once simmering, reduce the heat to low. Place the chocolate in the top pan or bowl and set it over the simmering water, making sure the pan or bowl sits high enough that the bottom doesn't touch the boiling water. Stir the chocolate continuously until it is completely melted and smooth and then remove from the heat.

## MELTING CHOCOLATE IN LIQUID

Chocolate can be safely melted in a liquid like cream, either in a saucepan or in a microwave-safe bowl in the microwave. In either case, chop the chocolate into small pieces (if not using chips or wafers) and use about 1 tablespoon of liquid per ounce of chocolate.

If using a saucepan, place the chocolate and liquid over medium heat and cook, stirring constantly, until the chocolate is completely melted and the mixture is smooth.

If using the microwave, combine the chocolate and liquid in a heat-safe bowl or measuring cup and microwave on high in 30-second intervals, stirring in between, until the chocolate is melted and the mixture is well combined.

# Mixing Liquid Ingredients

Mixing liquid ingredients may seem straightforward enough, but there are some specific techniques that will serve you well for mixing certain types of ingredients together. You'll commonly see the terms "cream," "cut in," and "fold" to refer to the process of combining liquid ingredients with either other liquid ingredients or nonliquid ingredients.

## CREAMING

A lot of baking recipes begin with the instruction to "cream together the butter and sugar." Creaming is a way of combining sugar and fat together in such a way that the sugar acts to aerate the fat, making cakes and other baked goods light and fluffy. Beating the butter (or other fat, such as shortening or lard) over and over with the grains of sugar creates tiny air bubbles within the fat.

To properly cream butter (or another fat) with sugar, always start with room-temperature butter. Combine the butter and sugar in a large mixing bowl and, using an electric mixer (either handheld or a stand mixer), beat on medium-high speed until the mixture is fluffy and becomes lighter in color. You'll need to stop the mixer at least once and scrape down the sides of the bowl using a rubber spatula. Creaming butter and sugar can be done by hand with a fork or wooden spoon but will take much more time and effort. Creaming with a mixer takes about 3 minutes.

## CUTTING IN

When making pastries like piecrusts, scones, and biscuits, fat is "cut in" to flour. To "cut in" means to distribute pea-size bits of fat throughout the flour. When these bits of fat melt as the pastry bakes in the oven, steam is created. The steam makes air pockets in the dough, which are responsible for the pastry's flakiness.

Fat can be cut into flour by either using a food processor or by hand using a pastry cutter, a fork, or two knives. The fat should be very cold to start and cut into small pieces.

**With a food processor:** Fit the processor with the steel "S" blade. Put the flour in the bowl of the processor and add the cold butter (or other fat). Pulse the processor in short bursts until the mixture resembles coarse meal with pea-size bits of fat distributed throughout the flour.

**By hand:** In a mixing bowl, combine the cold butter and flour. Use a pastry cutter, fork, or two knives to break the butter up into smaller and smaller bits, until there are pea-size bits of butter distributed throughout the flour.

## FOLDING

When you wish to mix a solid ingredient (such as fruit or nuts) with an airy, whipped liquid ingredient (like egg whites or whipped cream), you must be careful not to deflate the mixture. To do this, add the whipped or lighter ingredient to the heavier ingredient. Use a rubber spatula to gently lift the mixture from the bottom of the bowl and fold it on top of itself. Turn the bowl 45 degrees after each fold, until the ingredients are combined.

# Techniques for Eggs

Many dessert recipes rely on eggs—for binding, for silky richness, or for leavening. Some recipes call for whole eggs. Cookies, brownies, and cakes, for instance, benefit from both the fat in the yolks and the leavening qualities of the whites. Other recipes, like those for airy desserts like soufflé or meringue, require the lightness of egg whites that have been filled with air through whipping. Still others, like custards, rely on the fat of the yolks for a rich, smooth, dense consistency.

### WHIPPING EGG WHITES

Dishes like soufflé, mousse, and meringue are made fluffy and light by the addition of egg whites that have been whipped, or aerated.

To properly whip egg whites, start with the eggs at room temperature and use a large mixing bowl and a whisk, handheld electric mixer, or stand mixer fitted with the whisk attachment. Make sure that all equipment is clean and dry before beginning. If using a mixer, begin by beating at low speed until the whites become foamy. Increase the speed to medium or medium-high and continue to beat.

*Soft Peaks:* Egg whites are at the "soft peak" stage when they form mounds that flop over a little when you pull out the whisk or beater.

*Stiff Peaks:* The egg whites become smooth and glossy and form peaks that hold their shape when the whisk or beater is pulled out. Once the eggs have nearly reached the stiff peaks stage, adding a pinch of cream of tartar will stabilize them, helping them to maintain their airiness.

### TEMPERING EGGS

Before adding eggs to hot liquid, they need to be "tempered," or gently heated just enough so that the heat of the liquid won't immediately cook them (which would give the mixture a scrambled egg texture). To temper eggs, add about ¼ to ½ cup of hot liquid to the eggs while whisking continuously. This will bring the temperature of the egg closer to the temperature of the liquid without cooking them. Once the liquid has been incorporated into the eggs, you can add the mixture to the main pot of hot liquid, still whisking continuously to combine.

# Working with Pastry Dough

With a bit of knowledge and practice, making a good pastry crust is easily achieved. Before long you can create piecrusts, tart crusts, and pastries that are light, flaky, and beautifully golden brown and that hold their shape when baked.

## MAKING PASTRY DOUGH

Pastry dough might seem a bit intimidating if you've never attempted it, but follow these tips for perfect, flaky piecrusts and tart crusts every time.

1. ***Always start with butter (or other fat) that is very cold.*** Refrigerate it for several hours, or leave it in the freezer overnight.

2. ***Review the information about cutting butter into flour (see page 15).*** Sugar, salt, and other ingredients are added at this stage as well.

3. ***Add ice water a little at a time.*** Mix until the crumbly flour-and-butter mixture comes together in a dough ball.

4. ***Flatten the ball into a disk shape and wrap it tightly in plastic wrap.*** Refrigerate it for at least 30 minutes. Chilling firms up the fat in the dough, making it easy to handle. Cold butter or fat also makes the finished pastry flaky and tender.

## ROLLING OUT DOUGH

Remove the pastry dough from the refrigerator, unwrap it, and place it on a lightly floured work surface. Lightly dust the dough with flour. Using a heavy rolling pin, roll from the center of the dough away from your body. Lift the dough and turn it 90 degrees, then roll again from the center away from your body. Continue turning and rolling until the dough is the thickness and size required for the recipe. For a pie or tart crust, ⅛ inch is the perfect thickness.

To transfer a large piece of rolled-out dough to a pie or tart pan, roll it around the rolling pin and then unroll it onto the pan. Use your fingertips to gently push the dough into the bottom and corners of the pan. Use kitchen shears or a sharp knife to trim the excess dough that hangs over the sides of the pan.

## CRIMPING DOUGH

Crimping—in other words, folding or pinching—the edges of your pastry crust gives it a finished look. Once the dough is in the baking pan, press your index finger against the edge of the dough from the inside of the pan. With your thumb and index finger of the other hand pressed together to make a "V," push the dough around the tip of the other index finger from the outside. Do this all the way around, creating a scalloped edge.

## BLIND BAKING

Blind baking is prebaking, or partially baking, the crust of a pie or tart before adding the filling. Partially baking the crust prevents it from becoming soggy from a moist filling. Blind baking is also used for pies with uncooked fillings (like a banana cream pie), so you add the filling to a fully baked crust.

Without a filling to weight it down and hold the sides up, a crust can puff up or droop on the sides during blind baking. I recommend using pie weights (or an alternative like dried beans or rice) to prevent this. Line the crust with parchment paper or aluminum foil. Add the weights and then bake until the edges of the crust turn golden brown. For a partially baked crust, this should take 10 to 15 minutes. For a fully baked crust, bake about 5 minutes less, remove the weights, and continue to bake until the bottom is golden brown, 5 to 10 minutes more. If you don't have pie weights or a suitable alternative, you can "dock" the crust by poking holes all over the bottom of the unbaked crust with the tines of a fork. This helps prevent the crust from puffing up as it bakes, though it is not as effective as weights and won't keep the sides from drooping.

# Decorating

Baking cakes, cupcakes, and cookies is great fun, and decorating them with colorful frostings, icings, sprinkles, and other toppers is an added bonus. Here are some of the best methods for decorating your cakes and cookies.

## FROSTING CAKES AND CUPCAKES

Frosting can be used to create all sorts of fun visual effects. Color the cakes and cupcakes using gel food coloring, which comes in intense colors that require only a few drops to create a beautiful hue. Sprinkles of all shapes, sizes, and colors can be used to enhance the look even further.

Use a knife or spatula to spread frosting evenly over an entire cake. Or use a piping bag (or a sturdy resealable plastic bag with one corner snipped off) for a more controlled application.

With a piping bag, you can use piping tips in different shapes to create all sorts of looks including flowers, decorative borders, and other effects.

- To fill a pastry bag, snip off the tip and place whatever piping tip you plan to use inside so that it sticks out of the opening. Place the bag, tip down, in a tall glass or pitcher and fold the bag down over the sides. Use a rubber spatula to scoop the frosting into the bag, filling it no more than two-thirds full. Close the bag tightly, pushing out any air pockets, and secure the end with a twist tie or a rubber band.

- Hold the bag perpendicular to the surface of the cake or cupcake, with the tip about ½ inch above it. Squeeze the bag from the top. You may want to practice first on a plate or a piece of parchment paper. (You can scoop your practice attempts back into the piping bag when you are ready to decorate the cake.)

- When piping frosting onto cupcakes, always start at the outer edge of the cupcake and pipe the frosting in an outside-in spiral. When you reach the center, stop squeezing and pull the tip straight up and away from the top of the cupcake.

When frosting a layer cake, start by leveling off the cake layers (I use a serrated knife to cut off the top of each cake layer to make the surface flat). Stack the layers with frosting in between. Be sure to place the top layer upside down (so that the part that was the bottom during baking, which is smooth, is now on top).

Next, add a "crumb coat," a thin layer of frosting that is intended to seal in the crumbs so that they don't get mixed up in the main frosting layer, to keep your cake looking neat and tidy. Refrigerate the cake for 15 to 30 minutes to firm up the crumb coat.

Add the finishing frosting in a thick layer over the top and sides of the cake using a knife or rubber spatula. As a final touch, you can use a piping bag to add flourishes either all over the cake or just around the edges as a border.

## DECORATING COOKIES

Cookies are usually topped with icing, which is thinner than frosting and often made of powdered sugar and milk (or another liquid). Icing can also be colored with gel food coloring, and sprinkles and other decorative toppings can also be added.

As with frosting, you can use a piping bag or a resealable plastic bag with the tip cut off to pipe icing onto cookies. Because icing is thinner, you'll want to use a tip with a smaller opening. A plastic squeeze bottle can also be used to add icing details.

# Part Two

# *Recipes*

# 3

# COOKIES, BROWNIES, AND BARS

Double Chocolate Cookies

PAGE 29

*S*ometimes all you want is one outrageously delicious cookie (okay, maybe three if they're small). Sometimes a fudgy brownie, a nut-studded blondie, or a fruit-based bar is just the thing. The recipes in this chapter cover all types of cookies, brownies, and bars—and each makes just enough for two people (perhaps four if you are dainty eaters.) Simple cookies like Spicy Ginger Cookies, Toffee Pecan Sandies, and White Chocolate Butter Cookies provide the crunch and sweetness I crave in a cookie. Butterscotch Blondies, Caramel Swirl Brownies, and Blueberry Cheesecake Bars satisfy me when I want something more decadent. You'll find some of these recipes include just an egg yolk or just an egg white. Save the part of the egg you're not using for another recipe (check the index on page 189 to find recipes that use just the white or yolk).

The Very Best Chocolate Chip Cookies **24**

Flourless Peanut Butter Cookies **26**

Whole-Wheat Oatmeal Cookies with
   Dried Blueberries **27**

Spicy Ginger Cookies **28**

Double Chocolate Cookies **29**

Lemon Shortbread Cookies **30**

Coconut Almond Chocolate Chunk Cookies **31**

Toffee Pecan Sandies **32**

Mexican Wedding Cookies **33**

White Chocolate Butter Cookies **35**

Cocoa Cutout Cookies **36**

Mocha Meringue Kisses **37**

Butterscotch Blondies **38**

Classic Double Chocolate Brownies **39**

Coffee and Cream Brownies **40**

Caramel Swirl Brownies **42**

Lemon Bars with Toasted Almonds **43**

Apple Pie Bars **45**

Blueberry Cheesecake Bars **47**

Caramel Crumb Bars **48**

Red Velvet Layer Bars **50**

No-Bake Chocolate
   Peanut Butter Bars **51**

# The Very Best
# Chocolate Chip Cookies

**Makes 6 cookies • Prep time: 10 minutes • Cook time: 9 to 11 minutes • Quick**

I couldn't write a dessert cookbook without including a recipe for this quintessential cookie. It's the first cookie I ever made all by myself and the one I crave most often when I just want a little something sweet. I've been known to make a full batch, freeze the dough in cookie-size balls, and keep them in the freezer for a quick fix, but that involves serious advance planning. This recipe produces gooey, freshly baked, chocolate-studded cookies in about 20 minutes—and it makes just enough to satisfy two people who have been struck with a sudden craving.

½ cup all-purpose flour

¼ teaspoon baking soda

¼ teaspoon salt

¼ cup (½ stick) unsalted
   butter, melted

¼ cup light brown sugar

2 tablespoons
   granulated sugar

1 large egg yolk

½ teaspoon vanilla extract

⅓ cup semisweet
   chocolate chips

1. ***Preheat the oven and prepare the baking sheet.*** Preheat the oven to 350°F. Line the baking sheet with parchment paper.

2. ***Mix the dry ingredients.*** In a small bowl, stir together the flour, baking soda, and salt.

3. ***Mix the wet ingredients.*** In a medium bowl, combine the butter, brown sugar, and granulated sugar and stir until smooth. Add the egg yolk and vanilla and stir until the mixture is well combined.

**4. Combine the wet and dry ingredients.** Add the flour mixture to the butter-and-sugar mixture and stir to mix well. Stir in the chocolate chips.

**5. Form and bake the cookies.** Drop rounded tablespoons of the dough onto the prepared baking sheet, leaving at least 2 inches of space in between each spoonful. Bake for 9 to 11 minutes, until lightly browned. Let cool on the sheet.

## *Tip*

Push these cookies over the top by browning the butter before combining it with the sugars. Melt the butter in a saucepan over medium heat and then continue to cook, swirling the pan frequently. The butter will sizzle and become foamy and then the foam will subside. After a few minutes, the butter will begin to brown and give off a nutty aroma. Once the butter has turned an amber color, transfer it immediately to a medium mixing bowl. Let cool for a few minutes before adding the sugars.

# *Flourless Peanut Butter Cookies*

**Makes 6 cookies • Prep time: 10 minutes • Cook time: 10 minutes • Quick**

The only flavor that comes close to chocolate in my affections is peanut butter—so it's no surprise that a classic peanut butter cookie is high on my list of must-have recipes. This recipe is perfect for making in small batches because it uses pantry staples. As an added bonus, these cookies are also gluten free.

⅓ cup creamy peanut butter, at room temperature

⅓ cup sugar

1 large egg yolk

¼ teaspoon vanilla extract

¼ teaspoon baking soda

1. ***Preheat the oven and prepare the baking sheet.*** Preheat the oven to 350°F. Line the baking sheet with parchment paper. (The cookies have enough fat in them that you can skip using parchment paper if you prefer.)

2. ***Mix the ingredients.*** In a medium bowl, stir together the peanut butter and sugar until creamy and well combined. Add the egg yolk, vanilla, and baking soda and stir until smooth.

3. ***Form the cookies.*** Form the dough into six even balls and place them on the prepared baking sheet, leaving at least 2 inches of space in between each ball. Using the tines of a fork, press the balls flat and create the classic crisscross pattern.

4. ***Bake the cookies.*** Bake for about 10 minutes, until the edges of the cookies are set. Let the cookies cool on the sheet.

## *Tip*

Peanut butter and dark chocolate are an undeniably delicious combination, so you can't go wrong by adding chocolate chunks or chips to this cookie batter. Or try drizzling melted dark chocolate decoratively over the cookies after they've cooled.

# Whole-Wheat Oatmeal Cookies with Dried Blueberries

**Makes 6 cookies • Prep time: 10 minutes • Cook time: 9 to 11 minutes • Quick, Lightly Sweet**

Whole-wheat flour, wholesome oats, natural honey, and superfood blueberries turn a classic cookie into one even the Berkeley hippie parents of my childhood would appreciate. They're buttery with a nice chewy texture, and they have just the right level of sweetness.

| | | |
|---|---|---|
| ¼ cup (½ stick) unsalted butter, at room temperature | 1 large egg yolk | ¼ teaspoon baking soda |
| 3 tablespoons honey | ½ teaspoon vanilla | ¼ teaspoon cinnamon |
| 5 tablespoons light brown sugar | ½ cup whole-wheat flour | ⅛ teaspoon kosher salt |
| | ¾ cup old-fashioned rolled oats | ¼ cup dried blueberries |

1. **Preheat the oven and prepare the baking sheet.** Preheat the oven to 375°F. Line the baking sheet with parchment paper. (The cookies have enough fat in them that you can skip using parchment paper if you prefer.)

2. **Mix the wet ingredients.** In a medium bowl, using an electric mixer on medium-high, cream together the butter, honey, and sugar until light and fluffy, about 3 minutes. Add the egg yolk and vanilla and beat to incorporate well.

3. **Add the dry ingredients.** Add the flour, oats, baking soda, cinnamon, and salt and beat to combine. Using a rubber spatula, stir in the dried blueberries.

4. **Form the cookies.** Make six balls of dough (about 2 inches round) and arrange them on the prepared baking sheet, leaving at least 2 inches of space between each ball. Using your fingers or the flat bottom of a glass, press each ball down onto the baking sheet to flatten, about ½-inch thick.

5. **Bake the cookies.** Bake for 8 to 9 minutes, until the cookies begin to turn golden around the edges. Transfer the cookies to a wire rack to cool.

## Tip

To make perfectly portioned cookies, use a medium-size, spring-loaded cookie scoop.

# Spicy Ginger Cookies

EQUIPMENT/TOOLS: BAKING SHEET, PARCHMENT PAPER, ELECTRIC MIXER, WIRE RACK

**Makes 6 cookies • Prep time: 10 minutes • Cook time: 8 to 10 minutes • Quick**

With crisp edges and a chewy center, these spicy little cookies fall somewhere between traditional gingersnaps and gingerbread cookies. Whatever you call them, they are a perfect sweet treat after a large meal—ginger does aid digestion, after all—or alongside a cup of tea or a glass of cold milk.

¾ cup all-purpose flour

¾ teaspoon ground ginger

¼ teaspoon cinnamon

¼ teaspoon baking soda

⅛ teaspoon kosher salt

3 tablespoons unsalted butter, at room temperature

¼ cup light brown sugar

1½ tablespoons molasses

1 large egg white

2 tablespoons granulated sugar

1. ***Preheat the oven and prepare the baking sheet.*** Preheat the oven to 350°F. Line the baking sheet with parchment paper.

2. ***Mix the dry ingredients.*** In a medium bowl, whisk together the flour, ginger, cinnamon, baking soda, and salt.

3. ***Mix the wet ingredients.*** In another medium mixing bowl, use an electric mixer on medium-high to cream together the butter and brown sugar until light and fluffy, about 3 minutes. Add the molasses and egg white and beat for about 1 minute more.

4. ***Combine the wet and dry ingredients.*** Add the dry ingredients to the bowl with the wet ingredients and beat just until the dry ingredients are well combined. Do not overmix.

5. ***Form the cookies.*** Form the dough into six small balls. Place the granulated sugar in a small dish and roll each dough ball in the sugar to coat it all around. Arrange the balls on the prepared baking sheet, leaving at least 2 inches in between each ball.

6. ***Bake the cookies.*** Bake for 8 to 10 minutes, until the tops crackle and the edges are firm. Let the cookies cool on the sheet for a minute, then transfer them to a wire rack to cool completely.

## *Tip*

For an even more flavorful cookie, substitute 2 teaspoons of grated fresh ginger for the ground ginger.

# Double Chocolate Cookies

**Makes 6 cookies • Prep time: 10 minutes • Cook time: 10 minutes • Quick**

Chocolate lovers alert! These cookies are super chocolatey. A tall glass of cold milk on the side is practically a requirement. They're fantastic as a dessert on their own, but they make insanely good "bread" for Classic Ice Cream Sandwiches (page 180), too.

¼ cup (½ stick) unsalted butter, melted

¼ cup light brown sugar

2 tablespoons granulated sugar

1 large egg yolk

¾ teaspoon vanilla extract

½ cup all-purpose flour

1½ tablespoons unsweetened cocoa powder

¼ teaspoon baking soda

⅛ teaspoon kosher salt

½ cup semisweet chocolate chips

1. **Preheat the oven and prepare the baking sheet.** Preheat the oven to 350°F. Line the baking sheet with parchment paper.

2. **Mix the wet ingredients.** In a medium bowl, whisk together the butter, brown sugar, and granulated sugar. Add the egg yolk and vanilla and continue to whisk until well combined and smooth, about 1 minute.

3. **Mix the remaining ingredients.** In a separate medium bowl, stir together the flour, cocoa powder, baking soda, and salt. Add the dry ingredients to the wet ingredients and stir until just combined. Using a spoon or rubber spatula, fold in the chocolate chips.

4. **Form the cookies.** Form the dough into six balls and arrange them on the prepared baking sheet, leaving at least 3 inches of space between each ball. Using your fingers or the flat bottom of a glass, press the balls gently to flatten, ¼- to ½-inch thick.

5. **Bake the cookies.** Bake until the cookies are firm around the edges but still soft in the center, about 10 minutes. Let the cookies cool on the baking sheet for about 2 minutes, then transfer to a wire rack to cool completely.

## Tip

Add ⅛ teaspoon cayenne pepper along with the salt for a spicy kick.

# Lemon Shortbread Cookies

**Makes 6 to 8 cookies • Prep time: 10 minutes, plus 1 hour to chill •
Bake time: 20 to 25 minutes**

Buttery, crumbly, and with the tart bite of lemon, these cookies are addictive. I could eat a dozen of them easily—which is exactly why I love this small-batch version. I happily devour my allotted three cookies and my work is done, my sweet craving fully satisfied.

¼ cup (½ stick) unsalted butter, at room temperature

¼ cup confectioners' sugar

½ cup all-purpose flour

1 teaspoon freshly grated lemon zest

¼ teaspoon vanilla extract

Pinch kosher salt

1. **Make the dough.** In a food processor or using an electric mixer on medium-high, cream the butter and sugar together until well combined, about 3 minutes. Add the flour, lemon zest, vanilla, and salt and mix just until dough comes together in a smooth ball.

2. **Chill the dough.** Form the dough into a log about 3 inches in diameter and wrap it in plastic wrap. Chill in the refrigerator for at least 1 hour.

3. **Preheat the oven and form the cookies.** Preheat the oven to 300°F. Using a serrated knife, slice the chilled dough into six to eight rounds. Arrange the cookies on a baking sheet, leaving at least an inch between them.

4. **Bake the cookies.** Bake for 20 to 25 minutes, until the cookies begin to turn golden brown. Let the cookies cool on the baking sheet.

## Tip

You can alter the flavor of these shortbread cookies easily by adding or substituting various ingredients for the lemon zest. Try adding ½ teaspoon of dried lavender for a lemon-lavender version. Substitute orange or lime zest for the lemon. Or take a sharp turn and replace the zest with a tablespoon or two of minced candied ginger.

# Coconut Almond Chocolate Chunk Cookies

EQUIPMENT/TOOLS: BAKING SHEET, PARCHMENT PAPER, ELECTRIC MIXER, WIRE RACK

**Makes 12 cookies • Prep time: 10 minutes • Cook time: 9 to 12 minutes • Quick**

These small cookies are all about texture and flavor. They're loaded with sweet, chewy coconut, crunchy almonds, and rich chunks of dark chocolate. Six cookies might seem like a lot per person, but these are small. They're also extra tasty, so I'm pretty sure you're going to want to eat all six.

½ cup plus 1 tablespoon
 all-purpose flour

¼ teaspoon baking soda

⅛ teaspoon kosher salt

¼ cup (½ stick) unsalted butter,
 at room temperature

¼ cup granulated sugar

½ teaspoon vanilla extract

1 large egg white

¾ cup semisweet
 chocolate chunks

½ cup sweetened
 shredded coconut

⅓ cup sliced almonds

1. **Preheat the oven and prepare the baking sheet.** Preheat the oven to 375°F. Line the baking sheet with parchment paper.

2. **Mix the dry ingredients.** In small bowl, stir together the flour, baking soda, and salt.

3. **Mix the wet ingredients.** In a medium bowl, cream together the butter and sugar using an electric mixer on medium-high for about 3 minutes. Add the vanilla and egg white and beat until just incorporated.

4. **Add the dry ingredients to the wet.** Add the dry ingredients to the wet ingredients and beat until just blended. Using a rubber spatula, fold in the chocolate chunks, coconut, and almonds.

5. **Form and bake the cookies.** Using a tablespoon or a small cookie scoop, form 12 balls and arrange them on the prepared baking sheet. Make sure to leave at least 2 inches of space between the balls. Bake for 9 to 12 minutes, until the tops are golden brown. Let the cookies cool on the baking sheet for 5 to 10 minutes, then transfer them to a wire rack to cool completely.

## Tip

Leave out the chocolate chunks. Instead melt the chocolate in the microwave and dip the cooled coconut-almond cookies into the chocolate to coat.

# Toffee Pecan Sandies

**EQUIPMENT/TOOLS: BAKING SHEET, PARCHMENT PAPER, ELECTRIC MIXER, WIRE RACK**

**Makes 6 cookies • Prep time: 10 minutes • Cook time: 15 to 17 minutes • Quick**

I have been obsessed with sandies forever. There's just something about that sandy, crumbly texture that I can't get enough of. These are buttery, nutty, and have the added bonus of bits of crunchy, sticky toffee mixed in. The toffee bits are optional, but not for me. I'm nearly as obsessed with toffee as I am with sandies. These cookies are great for a small batch since they don't call for egg.

¼ cup (½ stick) unsalted butter, at room temperature

¼ cup light brown sugar

¾ teaspoon vanilla extract

⅛ teaspoon salt

½ cup all-purpose flour

½ cup chopped pecans

⅓ cup toffee bits (optional)

1. **Preheat the oven.** Preheat the oven to 350°F. Line the baking sheet with parchment paper.

2. **Mix the ingredients.** In a medium bowl, use an electric mixer on medium-high to cream together the butter and brown sugar until light and fluffy, about 3 minutes. Beat in the vanilla and salt. Gradually beat in the flour with the mixer on low speed. Using a rubber spatula, gently fold in the pecans and toffee bits (if using).

3. **Form and bake the cookies.** Roll the dough into six balls about 1½ inches in diameter. Arrange the balls on the prepared baking sheet with a few inches of space between them. Using your fingers or the flat bottom of a glass, press down on the balls to flatten, ¼- to ½-inch thick. Bake for 15 to 17 minutes, until lightly golden brown. Transfer the cookies to a wire rack to cool completely.

# Mexican Wedding Cookies

**Makes 6 cookies • Prep time: 10 minutes, plus 15 minutes to chill • Cook time: 10 to 12 minutes**

A rich, buttery dough gives these powdered sugar–coated cookies their melt-in-your-mouth texture. Without any egg to hold the dough together, they turn out delightfully crumbly. Ground almonds and a dash of cinnamon give these an authentic Mexican flavor. Or switch things up, leave out the cinnamon, and use pecans or walnuts in place of the almonds for Russian tea cakes.

2½ tablespoons unsalted butter, at room temperature

2 tablespoons confectioners' sugar, plus additional for rolling the cookies

⅛ teaspoon vanilla extract

Pinch kosher salt

¼ cup plus 1½ teaspoons all-purpose flour

⅛ teaspoon cinnamon

2½ tablespoons ground almonds

1. ***Mix the wet ingredients.*** In a medium bowl, use an electric mixer on medium-high to cream together the butter and confectioners' sugar until light and fluffy, about 3 minutes. Add the vanilla and salt and beat until well incorporated.

2. ***Add the dry ingredients.*** Add the flour and cinnamon and beat until just combined. Using a spoon or rubber spatula, stir in the ground almonds.

3. ***Chill the dough.*** Cover the bowl with plastic wrap and chill in the refrigerator for at least 15 minutes.

4. ***Preheat the oven and form the cookies.*** Preheat the oven to 350°F. Form the dough into six 1-inch balls and arrange them on a baking sheet, leaving at least 1 inch of space in between each ball.

➤

5. ***Bake the cookies.*** Bake for 10 to 12 minutes, until the bottoms of the cookies begin to turn golden brown. Let the cookies cool on the baking sheet on a wire rack for about 5 minutes.

6. ***Dust the cookies.*** Put a few tablespoons of confectioners' sugar in a small bowl. While the cookies are still warm but cool enough to handle, roll each cookie in the confectioners' sugar to coat. Set the cookies on the wire rack to cool completely.

## Tip

For even more flavor, toast the almonds before grinding them (in a coffee or spice grinder or food processor). Place a cup or so of whole almonds in a skillet over medium heat and toast, stirring frequently, until they begin to turn golden and become fragrant, 3 to 5 minutes.

# White Chocolate Butter Cookies

EQUIPMENT/TOOLS: FOOD PROCESSOR, PLASTIC WRAP,
BAKING SHEET, PARCHMENT PAPER, WIRE RACK

**Makes 6 cookies • Prep time: 10 minutes, plus 1 hour to chill •
Cook time: 15 minutes • Lightly Sweet**

These delicate, buttery cutout cookies are laced with the subtle flavor of white chocolate. Be sure to use a good quality white chocolate—the kind that is made with at least 20 percent cocoa butter. Both the flavor and texture of the cookies will benefit greatly from using "real" white chocolate over the kind made with vegetable oil.

| | | |
|---|---|---|
| 3 tablespoons all-purpose flour | Pinch kosher salt | ¼ teaspoon vanilla extract |
| 1½ tablespoons granulated sugar | 3 tablespoons unsalted butter, at room temperature | ¾ ounce white chocolate, finely chopped |

1. ***Mix the ingredients.*** In a food processor, add the flour, sugar, and salt and pulse a few times to combine. Add the butter and vanilla and pulse until the mixture resembles coarse meal. Add the chocolate and pulse to incorporate.

2. ***Chill the dough.*** Turn the dough mixture out onto a sheet of plastic wrap and press it together into a ball. Flatten the ball into a disk shape and wrap it tightly in the plastic wrap. Chill in the refrigerator for at least 1 hour.

3. ***Preheat the oven.*** Preheat the oven to 350°F. Line the baking sheet with parchment paper.

4. ***Form and bake the cookies.*** Roll the chilled dough out to an even ¼-inch thickness. Use a fluted, round, 3-inch cookie cutter to cut out six cookies. Arrange the cookies on the prepared baking sheet, leaving at least 2 inches of space between each cookie. Bake for about 15 minutes, until the edges turn golden brown. Transfer the cookies to a wire rack to cool completely.

## *Tip*

For a unique flavor twist, add ½ teaspoon of dried lavender (be sure to use culinary-grade lavender) along with the sugar.

# Cocoa Cutout Cookies

**Makes 8 cookies • Prep time: 10 minutes, plus 1 hour to chill •
Cook time: 16 to 18 minutes • Lightly Sweet**

These thin, crisp, wafer-like cookies pack big chocolate flavor. You can use any shape of cookie cutter you like—I use a 2½-inch round cutter to get 8 cookies. Your yield will vary depending on the size of the cutter you use. Use a heart-shaped cutter to make these into a lovely Valentine's Day treat.

¼ cup plus 2 tablespoons all-purpose flour, plus additional for rolling out the dough

2 tablespoons granulated sugar

2 tablespoons confectioners' sugar

1 tablespoon cornmeal

1½ tablespoons unsweetened cocoa powder

⅛ teaspoon kosher salt

Pinch baking soda

¼ cup (½ stick) cold unsalted butter, cut into small pieces

¼ teaspoon vanilla extract

1. ***Mix the ingredients.*** In a food processor, add the flour, granulated sugar, confectioners' sugar, cornmeal, cocoa powder, salt, and baking soda and pulse a few times to combine. Drop in the cold butter pieces and pulse until the mixture looks like wet sand. Add the vanilla and pulse until just incorporated.

2. ***Chill the dough.*** Turn out the dough onto a sheet of plastic wrap and pat it into a disk shape. Wrap the disk tightly in the plastic and chill in the refrigerator for at least 1 hour.

3. ***Preheat the oven and prepare the baking sheet.*** Preheat the oven to 325°F. Line the baking sheet with parchment paper.

4. ***Form and bake the cookies.*** On a lightly floured board or counter, roll out the dough into an even ¼-inch thickness. Use a cookie cutter to cut out the cookies. Arrange the cookies on the prepared baking sheet, leaving at least 2 inches of space between each cookie. Bake until the tops of the cookies are firm, 16 to 18 minutes. Let the cookies cool to room temperature on the baking sheet.

## Tip

Instead of using a cookie cutter, you can use a canning jar ring or a juice glass to cut out uniform-size cookies.

# Mocha Meringue Kisses

EQUIPMENT/TOOLS: BAKING SHEET, PARCHMENT PAPER,
ELECTRIC MIXER, PIPING BAG OR RESEALABLE BAG

**Makes 12 kisses • Prep time: 15 minutes • Cook time: 1 hour**

Shaped like classic Hershey's Kisses, these pillowy coffee-chocolate meringues are melt-in-your-mouth delicious. Serve them with a cup of coffee or hot cocoa, or even a shot of coffee-flavored liqueur.

2½ tablespoons confectioners' sugar

1 tablespoon unsweetened cocoa powder

¾ teaspoon cornstarch

¼ teaspoon instant espresso or coffee powder

1 large egg white

¼ teaspoon vanilla extract

Pinch cream of tartar

1 tablespoon granulated sugar

1. **Preheat the oven.** Preheat the oven to 250°F. Line the baking sheet with parchment paper.

2. **Mix the dry ingredients.** In a small bowl, whisk together the confectioners' sugar, cocoa powder, cornstarch, and espresso powder.

3. **Whip the egg white.** In a medium bowl, use an electric mixer on medium-high to beat the egg white, vanilla, and cream of tartar on high speed until soft peaks form, about 2 minutes. Add the granulated sugar and continue to beat until the mixture forms stiff peaks.

4. **Mix the dry ingredients into the whipped egg white.** Using a spoon or rubber spatula, gently fold the dry ingredients into the whipped egg white.

5. **Pipe the batter onto the baking sheet.** Transfer the mixture to a piping bag fitted with a ½-inch round tip. Holding the piping bag perpendicular to the prepared baking sheet, pipe the mixture into 12 peaks, each about the size of a Hershey's Kiss.

6. **Bake the cookies.** Bake for 1 hour. Let the meringues cool completely on the baking sheet.

## Tip

If you don't want to pipe the meringue onto the baking sheet, you can drop the mixture by heaping teaspoonfuls.

# Butterscotch Blondies

**Makes 4 blondies • Prep time: 10 minutes • Cook time: 25 to 30 minutes**

Calling blondies chocolate-free brownies fails to recognize what makes them so uniquely crave-worthy. Their flavor oomph comes from brown sugar. Use dark brown for the deepest flavor. It is delicious in its own right—deep, round, and caramelly. This recipe makes 4 round blondies, which means you can either have two per person or use them as the "bread" for a couple of irresistible Classic Ice Cream Sandwiches (page 180).

2 tablespoons unsalted butter, melted

¼ cup dark brown sugar

1 large egg yolk

¼ teaspoon vanilla extract

¼ cup all-purpose flour

⅛ teaspoon baking powder

Pinch baking soda

Pinch kosher salt

2 tablespoons butterscotch chips

1. ***Preheat the oven and prepare the muffin tin.*** Preheat the oven to 350°F. Grease 4 wells of a muffin tin with baking spray.

2. ***Mix the wet ingredients.*** In a medium bowl, whisk together the butter and brown sugar. Add the egg yolk and vanilla and whisk to combine well.

3. ***Add the dry ingredients.*** Add the flour, baking powder, baking soda, and salt and stir until just combined. Fold in the butterscotch chips.

4. ***Bake the blondies.*** Divide the batter evenly between the 4 prepared muffin tin wells. Bake until a toothpick inserted into the center comes out clean, 25 to 30 minutes. Let the blondies cool for 15 minutes before removing them from the tin.

## Tip

Use the 4 outside wells of the muffin tin for the most even baking.

# Classic Double Chocolate Brownies

EQUIPMENT/TOOLS: MUFFIN TIN, BAKING SPRAY

**Makes 2 brownies • Prep time: 10 minutes • Cook time: 30 minutes**

Classic fudgy brownies are probably my desert island dessert. They're easy to make, loaded with intense chocolate flavor, and impossible to eat in moderation when you're faced with an entire pan full of them. This downsized recipe is perfect. The resulting individually portioned brownies have a delightfully shiny and crackly top crust, and they're gooey, moist, and super chocolatey on the inside.

- 3 tablespoons granulated sugar
- 1 tablespoon unsalted butter
- Pinch kosher salt
- ¼ teaspoon vanilla extract

- 1½ tablespoons unsweetened cocoa powder
- 1 large egg yolk
- 1½ tablespoons all-purpose flour

- ⅛ teaspoon baking powder
- 2 tablespoons semisweet chocolate chips

1. **Preheat the oven and prepare the muffin tin.** Preheat the oven to 350°F. Grease 2 wells of a muffin tin with baking spray.

2. **Melt the butter with the sugar.** Combine the sugar, butter, and salt in a medium microwave-safe bowl. Heat in the microwave for 30 seconds and then stir. Return to the microwave and heat for another 30 seconds. Remove and stir again.

3. **Mix in the remaining ingredients.** Add the vanilla, cocoa powder, and egg yolk and stir until the mixture is well combined and glossy. Add the flour and baking powder and stir to incorporate. Stir in the chocolate chips.

4. **Bake the brownies.** Divide the batter between the prepared wells of the muffin tin. Bake for about 30 minutes. When done, the top should be firm, and a toothpick inserted into the center will come out clean. Let the brownies cool for 15 minutes before removing them from the tin.

## Tip

You can easily make these brownies gluten free by substituting your preferred gluten-free all-purpose flour mix for the all-purpose flour (and make sure that your baking powder and vanilla extract are gluten free as well).

# Coffee and Cream Brownies

**Makes 2 brownies · Prep time: 10 minutes · Cook time: 30 minutes**

Few flavors are so perfectly suited for each other as bitter coffee and sweet chocolate. This brownie recipe brings the two together by spiking both the brownie batter and a cream-cheese swirl with instant espresso powder. The result is heavenly. The recipe calls for using an egg yolk, so you can use the leftover egg white to make Mocha Meringue Kisses (page 37).

| | | |
|---|---|---|
| 1½ tablespoons unsalted butter | ¼ teaspoon vanilla extract | 1½ tablespoons all-purpose flour |
| 4 tablespoons granulated sugar, divided | 2 tablespoons instant espresso powder, divided | 1½ tablespoons cream cheese, at room temperature |
| Pinch kosher salt | 1½ tablespoons unsweetened cocoa powder | |
| 1 large egg yolk | | |

1. **Preheat the oven and prepare the muffin tin.** Preheat the oven to 350°F. Grease 2 wells of a muffin tin with baking spray.

2. **Melt the butter with the sugar.** Combine the butter with 3 tablespoons of the sugar and the salt in a medium microwave-safe bowl. Heat in the microwave for 30 seconds and then stir. Return to the microwave and heat for another 30 seconds. Remove and stir again.

3. **Mix in the remaining brownie batter ingredients.** Stir in the egg yolk and vanilla. Add 1 tablespoon of the espresso powder and the cocoa powder and stir until the mixture is well combined and glossy. Add the flour and stir to incorporate.

4. **Make the coffee cream swirl mixture.** In a small bowl, stir together the cream cheese with the remaining tablespoon of sugar and the remaining tablespoon of espresso powder.

5. ***Bake the brownies.*** Scoop two-thirds of the brownie batter into the prepared wells of the muffin tin, dividing evenly. Dollop the coffee cream mixture on top of the batter and then top with remaining brownie batter. Using a knife, swirl the brownie and cream mixtures together slightly, creating a swirling pattern. Bake for about 30 minutes. When done, the top should be firm, and a toothpick inserted into the center will come out clean. Let the brownies cool for 15 minutes before removing them from the tin.

## *Tip*

Instead of espresso powder, you can use a coffee-flavored liqueur like Kahlúa or Tia Maria. If you don't have any on hand and don't want to purchase a full-size bottle just for brownies, look for the mini airplane bottles at a discount liquor store.

# *Caramel Swirl Brownies*

**Makes 2 brownies • Prep time: 10 minutes, plus 1 hour to chill •
Cook time: 23 to 25 minutes**

These brownies are rich, sweet, chocolatey, and made all the more indulgent with a decadent swirl of caramel. You'll be glad you only made a two-serving batch, because these are impossible to stop eating (at least for me).

2½ tablespoons unsalted butter, at room temperature

¼ cup plus 1 tablespoon granulated sugar

Pinch kosher salt

1 large egg yolk

½ teaspoon vanilla extract

1½ tablespoons unsweetened cocoa powder

2 tablespoons all-purpose flour

3 tablespoons caramel sauce

1. ***Preheat the oven and prepare the muffin tin.*** Preheat the oven to 350°F. Grease 2 wells of a muffin tin with baking spray.

2. ***Melt the butter with the sugar.*** In a medium microwave-safe bowl, combine the butter, sugar, and salt. Heat in the microwave for 30 seconds and then stir. Return to the microwave and heat for another 30 seconds. Remove and stir again.

3. ***Mix in the remaining brownie batter ingredients.*** Stir in the egg yolk and vanilla. Add the cocoa powder and stir until the mixture is well combined and glossy. Add the flour and stir until just incorporated.

4. ***Bake the brownies.*** Scoop half of the brownie batter into the prepared muffin tin wells. Bake for 7 minutes. Spoon the caramel sauce on top of the brownies in the tin and then dollop the remaining brownie batter on top. Using a knife or toothpick, swirl the top two layers together. Continue to bake for 16 to 18 minutes more. Let cool to room temperature before chilling in the refrigerator for 1 hour.

## *Tip*

If you want to really put these brownies over the top, sprinkle them with pinches of flaky sea salt.

# *Lemon Bars with Toasted Almonds*

**EQUIPMENT/TOOLS: MINI LOAF PAN, PARCHMENT PAPER, PASTRY CUTTER**

**Makes 2 bars • Prep time: 10 minutes • Cook time: 35 minutes • Mini Equipment**

With their tart citrus flavor and bright yellow color, lemon bars are a refreshing departure from brownies. This version includes a crumbly shortbread-like crust that is simple to make and gets pressed right into the pan (no need for a rolling pin). The toasted almonds on top add a nice crunch and a welcome nuttiness that balances the sweet-tartness of the filling.

**FOR THE CRUST**

½ cup all-purpose flour

2 tablespoons
confectioners' sugar

¼ cup (½ stick) cold unsalted
butter, cut into small pieces

**FOR THE FILLING**

1 large egg

½ cup granulated sugar

Zest of 1 lemon

Juice of 1 lemon

1 tablespoon all-purpose flour

⅛ teaspoon baking powder

Pinch kosher salt

**FOR THE TOPPING**

2 tablespoons sliced almonds

1. ***Preheat the oven and prepare the pan.*** Preheat the oven to 350°F. Line your vessel of choice with parchment paper.

2. ***Make the crust.*** In a medium bowl, add the flour, confectioners' sugar, and butter. Using a pastry cutter, fork, or two knives, cut the butter into the flour and sugar until the mixture resembles coarse meal. Pour the mixture into the bottom of the prepared pan and pat it down into an even layer. Bake for 15 minutes, until lightly browned. Let cool in the pan for 10 minutes or so. Leave the oven on.

➤

3. ***Make the filling.*** In a small bowl, whisk together the egg, granulated sugar, lemon zest, and lemon juice. Add the flour, baking powder, and salt, and stir to incorporate. Pour the filling over the crust.

4. ***Bake the lemon bars.*** Bake for about 15 minutes. Scatter the almonds over the top of the filling. Return to the oven and bake for about 5 minutes more, until the filling is set and the almonds are golden brown. Let cool for 15 minutes before lifting out of the pan. Cut in half to serve.

## Equipment Hack

Use two widemouthed metal canning jar lids or two 4-ounce ramekins instead.

## Tip

You can make these bars gluten-free by substituting almond flour for the all-purpose flour in the filling. They'll have even more almond flavor, too.

# *Apple Pie Bars*

**EQUIPMENT/TOOLS: MINI LOAF PAN, PARCHMENT PAPER, PASTRY CUTTER**

**Makes 2 bars • Prep time: 10 minutes • Cook time: 33 to 35 minutes • Mini Equipment**

When you're craving a traditional streusel-topped apple pie but don't want to go to the trouble of baking an actual pie, this recipe is perfect. It has all the flavor of your favorite apple pie on top of a crumbly, buttery, shortbread-style crust.

**FOR THE CRUST**

½ cup all-purpose flour

2 tablespoons confectioners' sugar

¼ cup (½ stick) cold unsalted butter, cut into small pieces

**FOR THE FILLING**

2 Granny Smith apples, peeled, cored, and diced

1½ teaspoons freshly squeezed lemon juice

1 tablespoon granulated sugar

¼ teaspoon cinnamon

Pinch nutmeg

**FOR THE STREUSEL TOPPING**

2 tablespoons all-purpose flour

1½ tablespoons light brown sugar

1 tablespoon unsalted butter, at room temperature

1. ***Preheat the oven and prepare the pan.*** Preheat the oven to 350°F. Line your vessel of choice with parchment paper.

2. ***Make the crust.*** In a medium bowl, add the flour, confectioners' sugar, and butter. Using a pastry cutter, fork, or two knives, cut the butter into the flour and sugar until the mixture resembles coarse meal. Pour the mixture into the bottom of the prepared pan and pat it down into an even layer. Bake for 15 minutes, until lightly browned. Remove from the oven, leaving the oven on.

3. ***Make the filling.*** In a medium bowl, toss the apples with the lemon juice and then add the granulated sugar, cinnamon, and nutmeg and toss to mix well. Spread the topping over the crust.

4. ***Make the streusel topping.*** In a small bowl, stir together the flour, brown sugar, and butter with a fork. Mix until the mixture begins to resemble coarse meal. Spread the topping over the apples.

5. ***Bake the bars.*** Bake for 18 to 20 minutes, until the topping is golden brown and the apples are soft and bubbling. Let cool completely in the pan. Lift the bar out of the pan and cut in half to serve.

## Equipment Hack

Use two widemouthed metal canning jar lids or two 4-ounce ramekins instead.

## Tip

For a bit of added crunch and flavor, add 2 tablespoons of toasted, chopped pecans to the streusel mixture.

# Blueberry Cheesecake Bars

**Makes 2 bars • Prep time: 10 minutes, plus 4 hours to chill •
Cook time: 1 hour • Mini Equipment**

A sweet, crunchy graham cracker crust is topped with a layer of smooth, rich cheesecake with pops of juicy blueberries. You can freeze this cheesecake, tightly wrapped in plastic wrap, for up to 3 months. To serve, let thaw in the refrigerator overnight.

### FOR THE CRUST
⅓ cup graham cracker crumbs
  (about 2 full cracker sheets)
1 tablespoon unsalted
  butter, melted
1 teaspoon granulated sugar

### FOR THE FILLING
4 ounces cream cheese, at
  room temperature
2 tablespoons
  granulated sugar
1 large egg yolk

¼ teaspoon vanilla extract
⅓ cup fresh or
  frozen blueberries

1. ***Prepare the oven and pan.*** Place the oven rack in the lower third of the oven. Preheat the oven to 325°F. Line your vessel of choice with parchment paper.

2. ***Make the crust.*** In a small bowl, stir together the graham cracker crumbs, butter, and sugar. The mixture should be the texture of wet sand. Press the mixture firmly into the bottom of the prepared pan. Bake for about 20 minutes, until the top and edges are golden brown.

3. ***Make the filling.*** In a medium bowl, using an electric mixer on medium-high, beat together the cream cheese and sugar until smooth, about 3 minutes. Add the egg yolk and vanilla and beat to incorporate. Using a rubber spatula, fold in the blueberries.

4. ***Bake the cheesecake bars.*** Pour the filling over the crust and spread it into an even layer with a rubber spatula. Bake until the filling is set, 35 to 40 minutes. Cool the bars in the pan on a wire rack to room temperature, then chill in the refrigerator for at least 4 hours. Lift the cheesecake out of the pan and cut in half to serve.

## Equipment Hack

Use two widemouthed metal canning jar lids or two 4-ounce ramekins instead.

# *Caramel Crumb Bars*

EQUIPMENT/TOOLS: **MINI LOAF PAN, PARCHMENT PAPER, PASTRY CUTTER, SAUCEPAN**

**Makes 2 bars • Prep time: 10 minutes • Cook time: 35 minutes • Mini Equipment**

With a shortbread crust, a rich caramel filling, and a crumbly streusel topping, these bars are one of my favorite homemade desserts. You'll use a partial can of sweetened condensed milk, but save the rest (in an airtight container either in the refrigerator for a week or so or in the freezer for up to 3 months) and use it to make the ice cream for the Vietnamese Iced Coffee Float (page 174) or Red Velvet Layer Bars (page 50).

**FOR THE CRUST AND TOPPING**

½ cup plus 2 tablespoons
   all-purpose flour, divided
2 tablespoons
   granulated sugar
¼ cup (½ stick) cold unsalted
   butter, cut into small pieces

**FOR THE FILLING**

1 tablespoon unsalted butter
2 tablespoons dark
   brown sugar
⅓ cup sweetened
   condensed milk

1. ***Prepare the oven and pan.*** Place the oven rack in the lowest position. Preheat the oven to 350°F. Line your vessel of choice with parchment paper.

2. ***Make the crust and topping.*** In a medium bowl, add ½ cup of flour, the granulated sugar, and butter. Using a pastry cutter, fork, or two knives, cut the butter into the flour until the mixture resembles coarse meal. Pour three-quarters of the mixture into the bottom of the prepared pan and pat it down into an even layer. Bake for 10 minutes, until lightly browned. Remove from the oven (leave the oven on). While the crust bakes, add the remaining 2 tablespoons of flour to the remaining crust mixture and work it by hand until it again resembles coarse meal. Set aside.

3. ***Make the filling.*** In a small saucepan over medium heat, combine the butter, brown sugar, and sweetened condensed milk and heat, stirring occasionally, until the mixture comes to a boil. Reduce the heat as needed to keep the mixture at a gentle boil, until it thickens, about 10 minutes. Remove the pan from the heat and let cool for 5 minutes.

4. ***Fill and bake.*** Pour the cooled filling mixture over the crust, then sprinkle the topping mixture over the filling. Bake until the filling bubbles gently and is a deep caramel color and the crust and crumb topping are baked through. Let cool in the pan on a wire rack. Lift the bars out of the pan and cut in half to serve.

## Equipment Hack

Use two widemouthed metal canning jar lids or two 4-ounce ramekins instead.

## Tip

If you want to save time (and have one less dish to wash), substitute about ½ cup of caramel sauce or topping for the filling mixture.

# Red Velvet Layer Bars

**Makes 2 bars • Prep time: 10 minutes • Cook time: 35 minutes • Mini Equipment**

These magical layered bars have a red velvet cookie base, a welcome change from the more common graham cracker crust. The toppings—shredded coconut, chocolate chips, sweetened condensed milk, and pecans—form the classic layers. I like to use a natural food coloring or, if possible, just a spoonful of red beet juice to get the classic red velvet hue.

¼ cup plus 1 tablespoon all-purpose flour

1 teaspoon unsweetened cocoa powder

⅛ teaspoon baking powder

Pinch kosher salt

2 tablespoons unsalted butter, at room temperature

3 tablespoons granulated sugar

1 large egg yolk

¼ teaspoon vanilla extract

A few drops red gel food coloring

¼ cup sweetened shredded coconut

⅓ cup semisweet chocolate chips

⅓ cup sweetened condensed milk

¼ cup chopped pecans

1. *Preheat the oven and prepare the pan.* Preheat the oven to 350°F. Line your vessel of choice with parchment paper.

2. *Make the red velvet cookie layer.* In a medium bowl, whisk together the flour, cocoa powder, baking powder, and salt. In a separate medium bowl, cream the butter and sugar together with an electric mixer on medium-high until light and fluffy, about 3 minutes. Add the egg yolk and vanilla and beat to combine. Stir in the food coloring. Add the dry ingredients to the wet and beat to mix. Spread the cookie batter in the prepared pan and bake for 7 minutes. Remove the pan from the oven (leave the oven on).

3. *Assemble and bake.* Sprinkle the coconut and chocolate chips over the cookie layer. Pour the sweetened condensed milk over the top. Top with the pecans. Bake for 20 minutes. Let cool completely in the pan on a wire rack. Lift the bar out of the pan and cut in half.

## Equipment Hack

Use two widemouthed metal canning jar lids or two 4-ounce ramekins instead.

# No-Bake Chocolate Peanut Butter Bars

**Makes 2 bars • Prep time: 5 minutes, plus 20 minutes to chill •
Quick, No-Bake, Mini Equipment**

A sweet, creamy peanut butter layer studded with crunchy bits of graham crackers is topped with a layer of dark chocolate to make a heavenly treat. If you use a sweetened peanut butter, you might want to reduce the sugar in the recipe a bit.

1 tablespoon unsalted butter, melted

3 tablespoons graham cracker crumbs (1½ sheets)

3 tablespoons confectioners' sugar

2 tablespoons plus 1 teaspoon creamy peanut butter, divided

3 tablespoons semisweet chocolate chips

1. **Prepare the pan.** Line your vessel of choice with parchment paper.

2. **Make the peanut butter layer.** In a small bowl, stir together the butter, graham cracker crumbs, sugar, and 2 tablespoons of peanut butter and mix well. Transfer the mixture to the prepared pan and spread it into an even layer. Chill in the freezer for 5 minutes.

3. **Make the chocolate layer.** In a small microwave-safe bowl, combine the chocolate chips and the remaining 1 teaspoon of peanut butter. Heat for 30 to 45 seconds. Stir until the chocolate is completely melted and the mixture is well combined. Pour this over the peanut butter layer in the pan.

4. **Chill.** Freeze for 15 minutes or refrigerate for an hour before serving.

## Equipment Hack

Use two widemouthed metal canning jar lids or two 4-ounce ramekins instead.

# 4
# CUPCAKES AND CAKES

Mini Confetti Cakes

**PAGE 77**

**B**ecause sometimes a whole cake is just too many servings, the universe has provided us with the perfect alternative—cupcakes. These single-serving cakes are just the right size for one person. The recipes here make enough batter for two cupcakes. Some are traditional cupcakes, like Classic Vanilla Cupcakes with Buttercream or Salted Caramel Cupcakes made in a regular muffin tin, while others are simply downsized cakes cooked in mini cooking vessels like ramekins (Molten Lava Cakes, page 78) and coffee mugs (Chocolate-Hazelnut Mug Cakes, page 79).

Classic Vanilla Cupcakes with Buttercream **54**

Apples and Honey Cupcakes with Cinnamon Buttercream **56**

Marshmallow-Filled Chocolate Cupcakes **58**

Coconut Cupcakes with Coconut Buttercream **60**

Salted Caramel Cupcakes **62**

Spiced Chai Cupcakes **64**

Mimosa Cupcakes with Champagne-Orange Buttercream **66**

Mini Pumpkin Cheesecakes **68**

No-Bake Tiramisu Cheesecakes **69**

Coffee Crumb Cake **71**

Blueberry Yogurt Cake **73**

Mini Pineapple Upside-Down Cakes **74**

Mini Carrot Cakes **75**

Mini Confetti Cakes **77**

Molten Lava Cakes **78**

Chocolate-Hazelnut Mug Cakes **79**

Red Velvet Mug Cakes **80**

Peanut Butter Banana Cakes **81**

S'mores Cakes **82**

Graham Cracker Lime Icebox Cake **84**

Lemon Pudding Cakes **85**

# Classic Vanilla Cupcakes with Buttercream

EQUIPMENT/TOOLS: MUFFIN TIN, PAPER CUPCAKE LINERS, ELECTRIC MIXER, WIRE RACK

**Makes 2 cupcakes • Prep time: 10 minutes • Cook time: 15 to 17 minutes • Quick**

A simple vanilla cupcake topped with vanilla buttercream is a thing of beauty. It runs the risk of being overlooked for its plainness, but the delicate sweetness and floral flavor of vanilla in a fluffy, handheld cake topped with sweet, creamy frosting makes it a true classic. It's the simple things in life that make it so sweet.

**FOR THE CUPCAKES**

¼ cup all-purpose flour

¼ teaspoon baking powder

Pinch kosher salt

2 tablespoons unsalted butter, at room temperature

2½ tablespoons granulated sugar

1 large egg white

½ teaspoon vanilla extract

1½ tablespoons milk

**FOR THE BUTTERCREAM**

1½ tablespoons unsalted butter, at room temperature

½ cup confectioners' sugar

1½ teaspoons milk

Pinch kosher salt

¼ teaspoon vanilla extract

1 drop gel food coloring (optional)

Sprinkles or other decorations (optional)

1. ***Preheat the oven and prepare the muffin tin.*** Preheat the oven to 350°F. Line 2 wells of the muffin tin with paper cupcake liners.

2. ***Mix the dry ingredients.*** In a medium bowl, whisk together the flour, baking powder, and salt.

3. ***Mix the wet ingredients.*** In a separate medium bowl, beat the butter and sugar together with an electric mixer on medium-high until light and fluffy, about 3 minutes. Add the egg white and beat to incorporate. Stir in the vanilla.

4. ***Add the dry ingredients to the wet.*** Add half of the dry ingredients to the wet and beat until incorporated. Add the milk and mix to incorporate, then add the remaining dry ingredients and beat until just incorporated.

5. ***Bake the cupcakes.*** Divide the batter between the lined wells, making sure not to fill each more than two-thirds full. Bake for 15 to 17 minutes, until a toothpick inserted into the center comes out clean. Let cool in pan for a couple of minutes, and then transfer the cupcakes in their liners to a wire rack to cool completely.

6. ***Make the frosting.*** Using the electric mixer on medium-high, beat the butter until it is creamy, about 3 minutes. Add the confectioners' sugar, milk, salt, vanilla, and food coloring (if using) and beat until the mixture is thick and well combined.

7. ***Decorate the cupcakes.*** Once the cupcakes are completely cooled, pipe or spread the frosting on top. Add any sprinkles or other decorations you fancy (if using). Serve.

# *Apples and Honey Cupcakes with Cinnamon Buttercream*

**EQUIPMENT/TOOLS: MUFFIN TIN, PAPER CUPCAKE LINERS, ELECTRIC MIXER, WIRE RACK, PLASTIC WRAP**

**Makes 2 cupcakes** • **Prep time: 15 minutes** • **Cook time: 20 minutes** • **Lightly Sweet**

Sweetened with honey, apple, and just a touch of brown sugar, these charming little cupcakes are sweeter than muffins, but not as sweet as the typical cupcake. Even the buttercream frosting goes light on the sugar. These are delicious any time of year, but are especially perfect in the fall when apples are at their peak. I like to make these for Rosh Hashanah (the Jewish New Year), which happens to coincide with the fall apple season, because apples and honey are eaten to symbolize a sweet new year.

**FOR THE CUPCAKES**

2 tablespoons honey

1½ tablespoons unsalted butter, at room temperature

1½ tablespoons dark brown sugar

1 large egg white

½ cup all-purpose flour

¼ teaspoon baking soda

Pinch kosher salt

1 small apple, peeled, cored, and diced

**FOR THE FROSTING**

2 tablespoons all-purpose flour

3 tablespoons granulated sugar

3 tablespoons milk

3 tablespoons unsalted butter, at room temperature

¼ teaspoon vanilla extract

¼ teaspoon cinnamon

1. ***Preheat the oven and prepare the muffin tin.*** Preheat the oven to 325°F. Line 2 wells of the muffin tin with paper cupcake liners.

2. ***Mix the wet ingredients.*** In a medium bowl, use an electric mixer on medium to beat together the honey, butter, brown sugar, and egg white, about 2 minutes.

3. ***Add the dry ingredients.*** In a small bowl, whisk together the flour, baking soda, and salt. Add the dry mixture to the wet mixture and beat until just incorporated. Using a spoon or rubber spatula, fold in the diced apple.

**4. Bake the cupcakes.** Divide the batter between the lined wells, making sure not to fill each more than two-thirds full. Bake for about 20 minutes, until toothpick inserted into the center comes out clean. Let cool in pan for a couple of minutes, and then transfer the cupcakes in their liners to a wire rack to cool completely.

**5. Make the frosting.** In a small saucepan over medium-low heat, whisk together the flour and sugar. Add the milk and bring to a boil, whisking constantly, over medium-low heat. Cook, stirring constantly, for about 1 minute, until the mixture thickens. Remove the pan from the heat. Transfer the mixture to a small bowl and cover with plastic wrap. Refrigerate for about 20 minutes. In a small bowl, use the electric mixer on medium-high to beat the butter until it is light and fluffy, about 3 minutes. Add the cooled flour mixture. Beat until well combined and fluffy. Stir in the vanilla and cinnamon.

**6. Decorate the cupcakes.** Pipe or spread the frosting onto the cooled cupcakes and serve.

# Marshmallow-Filled Chocolate Cupcakes

EQUIPMENT/TOOLS: MUFFIN TIN, PAPER CUPCAKE LINERS, WIRE RACK

**Makes 2 cupcakes • Prep time: 15 minutes • Cook time: 16 minutes**

These chocolate cupcakes are hiding a sweet surprise: a gooey marshmallow that's baked right into the middle. A simple chocolate ganache is all you need to finish these off—it adds both intense chocolate flavor and a striking finished look.

**FOR THE CUPCAKES**

2 tablespoons all-purpose flour

1½ tablespoons cocoa powder

¼ teaspoon baking powder

Pinch kosher salt

2 tablespoons granulated sugar

1 tablespoon plus 1 teaspoon vegetable oil

1 large egg white

1 tablespoon milk

2 marshmallows

**FOR THE CHOCOLATE GANACHE**

1 tablespoon heavy (whipping) cream

2 tablespoons chopped semisweet chocolate

1. **Preheat the oven and prepare the muffin tin.** Preheat the oven to 350°F. Line 2 wells of the muffin tin with paper cupcake liners.

2. **Make the cupcake batter.** In a small bowl, whisk together the flour, cocoa powder, baking powder, and salt. In a medium bowl, whisk together the sugar, oil, egg white, and milk. Add the flour mixture and whisk to combine well.

3. **Bake the cupcakes.** Divide the batter between the lined wells, making sure not to fill each more than two-thirds full. Press one marshmallow into the center of each, submerging it in the batter. Bake for about 16 minutes. Let cool in the tin for a few minutes, and then transfer the cupcakes in their liners to a wire rack to cool completely.

**4. Make the ganache.** In a microwave-safe bowl, combine the cream and chocolate. Heat in the microwave in 30-second intervals on 60 percent power, stirring in between, until the chocolate is completely melted and the mixture is smooth.

**5. Glaze the cupcakes.** Dip the top of each cupcake into the ganache to coat the top. Let the ganache set for 5 minutes before serving.

## *Tip*

You can decorate these cupcakes to look just like those store-bought filled chocolate cupcakes you might remember from your childhood. In a small bowl, whisk together 2 tablespoons of confectioners' sugar and 1 teaspoon of milk. Put the mixture in a small plastic bag and snip off a small bit of one corner. Pipe a curlicue across the middle of each cupcake.

# Coconut Cupcakes with Coconut Buttercream

EQUIPMENT/TOOLS: MUFFIN TIN, ELECTRIC MIXER,
PAPER CUPCAKE LINERS, WIRE RACK

**Makes 2 cupcakes • Prep time: 10 minutes • Cook time: 15 to 17 minutes • Quick**

I am crazy for coconut. These cupcakes are my dessert fantasy come to life—fluffy little cakes laced with chewy, sweet threads of coconut and topped with a coconut buttercream frosting and even more sweetened shredded coconut. I'll even admit that I always double this recipe (using 1 whole egg). One of these cupcakes is just not enough for me, and my son insists that I share.

**FOR THE CUPCAKES**

¼ cup all-purpose flour

¼ teaspoon baking powder

Pinch kosher salt

2 tablespoons butter, at room temperature

2½ tablespoons granulated sugar

1 large egg white

½ teaspoon coconut extract

1½ tablespoons full-fat coconut milk

2 tablespoons sweetened shredded coconut

**FOR THE BUTTERCREAM**

1½ tablespoons unsalted butter, at room temperature

½ cup confectioners' sugar

1½ teaspoons coconut milk

¼ teaspoon coconut extract

2 tablespoons sweetened shredded coconut

1. ***Preheat the oven and prepare the muffin tin.*** Preheat the oven to 350°F. Line 2 wells of the muffin tin with paper cupcake liners.

2. ***Mix the cupcake dry ingredients.*** In a small bowl, combine the flour, baking powder, and salt.

3. ***Mix the cupcake wet ingredients.*** In a medium bowl, use an electric mixer on medium-high to beat the butter and sugar together until light and fluffy, about 3 minutes. Add the egg white and beat to incorporate. Stir in the coconut extract.

4. ***Add the dry ingredients to the wet.*** Add half of the dry ingredients to the wet and beat until just incorporated. Stir in the coconut milk. Add the remaining dry ingredients and beat until just incorporated. Using a spoon or rubber spatula, fold in the coconut.

5. ***Bake the cupcakes.*** Divide the batter between the lined wells, making sure not to fill each more than two-thirds full. Bake for 15 to 17 minutes, until a toothpick inserted into the center comes out clean. Let cool in the tin for a couple of minutes, then transfer the cupcakes in their liners to a wire rack to cool completely.

6. ***Make the buttercream.*** In a small bowl, use the electric mixer on medium-high to beat the butter until it is creamy, about 2 minutes. Add the confectioners' sugar, coconut milk, and coconut extract and beat until the mixture is thick and well combined.

7. ***Decorate the cupcakes.*** Once the cupcakes are completely cooled, pipe or spread the frosting on top. Press the shredded coconut into the frosting and serve.

## *Tip*

For added flavor and color, sprinkle toasted coconut on top of the cupcakes after frosting them. To toast the coconut, spread it on a baking sheet and toast it in a 325°F oven for about 5 minutes, until golden brown.

# Salted Caramel Cupcakes

EQUIPMENT/TOOLS: MUFFIN TIN, PAPER CUPCAKE LINERS, ELECTRIC MIXER, WIRE RACK, SAUCEPAN

**Makes 2 cupcakes • Prep time: 10 minutes • Bake time: 20 to 22 minutes**

Salted caramel may be trendy, but it will never get old for me. I will never stop craving that salty-sweet flavor combo. The cupcakes here get caramel flavor from a brown sugar cake and a luscious caramel buttercream. A dusting of flaky sea salt over the top balances all that sweetness beautifully.

## FOR THE CUPCAKES

¼ cup all-purpose flour

¼ teaspoon baking powder

Pinch kosher salt

1½ tablespoons unsalted butter, at room temperature

2 teaspoons granulated sugar

1½ tablespoons dark brown sugar

¼ teaspoon vanilla extract

1 large egg white

1 tablespoon plus 1 teaspoon milk

## FOR THE FROSTING

1½ tablespoons unsalted butter, at room temperature

3 tablespoons dark brown sugar

1½ tablespoons milk or heavy (whipping) cream

Pinch kosher salt

¼ cup plus 2 tablespoons confectioners' sugar

Flaky sea salt, for sprinkling

1. ***Preheat the oven and prepare the muffin tin.*** Preheat the oven to 350°F. Line 2 wells of the muffin tin with paper cupcake liners.

2. ***Make the cupcake batter.*** In a small bowl, combine the flour, baking powder, and salt. In a medium bowl, use an electric mixer on medium-high to cream together the butter, granulated sugar, and brown sugar until light and fluffy, about 3 minutes. Add the vanilla and egg white and beat to combine. Add half the dry ingredients and beat until just incorporated. Stir in the milk, then add the remaining dry ingredients and beat until just incorporated.

3. ***Bake the cupcakes.*** Divide the batter between the lined wells, making sure not to fill each more than two-thirds full. Bake for 16 to 18 minutes, until a toothpick inserted into the center comes out clean. Let cool in the tin for a few minutes, then transfer the cupcakes in their liners to a wire rack to cool completely.

4. ***Make the frosting.*** In a small saucepan over medium heat, combine the butter, brown sugar, cream, and salt and cook, stirring constantly, until the sugar has dissolved completely, about 4 minutes. Transfer the mixture to a medium bowl and let cool. When cool, add the confectioners' sugar and stir until the mixture thickens and reaches your desired consistency.

5. ***Decorate the cupcakes.*** Once the cupcakes are completely cooled, pipe or spread the frosting onto them. Sprinkle with the flaky sea salt before serving.

## *Tip*

If your frosting won't hold its shape, pop it in the fridge for 10 minutes or so to stiffen up.

# Spiced Chai Cupcakes

EQUIPMENT/TOOLS: MUFFIN TIN, PAPER CUPCAKE LINERS, SAUCEPAN, ELECTRIC MIXER, WIRE RACK

**Makes 2 cupcakes • Prep time: 10 minutes • Cook time: 25 minutes**

Spiced chai is a heady mixture of black tea, cinnamon, ginger, clove, cardamom, and black pepper. The flavor is spicy and big and beautifully mellowed with a splash of milk or cream and sugar. Infusing the flavor into a cupcake is pure genius. You may never be able to drink a regular cup of spiced chai again—it just makes me crave one of these little gems.

### FOR THE CUPCAKES

2 tablespoons plus
  2 teaspoons milk

1 spiced chai bag

2 tablespoons plus
  2 teaspoons all-purpose flour

⅛ teaspoon baking powder

Pinch baking soda

Pinch kosher salt

2 tablespoons
  granulated sugar

1 tablespoon plus
  1 teaspoon unsalted butter,
  at room temperature

1 large egg white

### FOR THE FROSTING

1½ tablespoons unsalted
  butter, at room temperature

½ cup confectioners' sugar

1½ teaspoons milk

¼ teaspoon cinnamon

Pinch kosher salt

1. ***Preheat the oven and prepare the muffin tin.*** Preheat the oven to 350°F. Line 2 wells of the muffin tin with paper cupcake liners.

2. ***Make the tea infusion.*** In a small saucepan over medium heat, heat the milk. When the milk begins to bubble, remove the pan from the heat and add the tea bag. Let stand for 10 minutes to let the tea infuse the milk. Remove and discard the tea bag.

3. ***Make the cupcake batter.*** In a small bowl, stir together the flour, baking powder, baking soda, and salt. In a medium bowl, use an electric mixer on medium to beat the tea-infused milk, granulated sugar, and butter until smooth, about 2 minutes. Add the egg white and beat to combine. Add the dry ingredients and beat to incorporate.

**4. *Bake the cupcakes.*** Divide the batter between the lined wells, making sure not to fill each more than two-thirds full. Bake for about 20 minutes, until toothpick inserted into the center comes out clean. Let cool in the tin for a few minutes, then transfer the cupcakes in their liners to a wire rack to cool completely.

**5. *Make the frosting.*** In a small bowl, use the electric mixer on medium-high to beat the butter until it is creamy, about 3 minutes. Add the confectioners' sugar, milk, cinnamon, and salt and beat until the mixture is thick and well combined.

**6. *Decorate the cupcakes.*** When the cupcakes are completely cooled, pipe or spread the frosting on top. Serve.

## *Tip*

If you don't have spiced chai bags, you can create your own chai flavor by adding pinches of all the requisite spices—cinnamon, ginger, clove, cardamom, and black pepper—to a mixture of black tea and milk.

# Mimosa Cupcakes with Champagne-Orange Buttercream

EQUIPMENT/TOOLS: MUFFIN TIN, PAPER CUPCAKE LINERS, ELECTRIC MIXER, WIRE RACK

**Makes 2 cupcakes · Prep time: 10 minutes · Cook time: 20 minutes · Quick**

As much as I love champagne, I've never been a day drinker, so you won't see me ordering a mimosa at brunch. These mimosa-flavored cupcakes, though, are a great way to celebrate any time of day. A splash of orange juice, a grating of zest, and a few glugs of sparkling wine and these cupcakes make any moment an occasion. You can serve the remaining champagne along with the cupcakes, or use it to make Strawberry Champagne Granita (page 173).

**FOR THE CUPCAKES**

¼ cup all-purpose flour

¼ teaspoon baking powder

Pinch kosher salt

1½ tablespoons unsalted butter, at room temperature

2 tablespoons plus 2 teaspoons granulated sugar

¼ teaspoon vanilla extract

1 large egg white

2 tablespoons plus 2 teaspoons champagne or other sparkling wine

1 teaspoon grated orange zest

2 teaspoons freshly squeezed orange juice

**FOR THE FROSTING**

1½ tablespoons unsalted butter, at room temperature

½ cup plus 2½ tablespoons confectioners' sugar

2 teaspoons champagne

1 teaspoon orange zest

2 teaspoons freshly squeezed orange juice

Pinch kosher salt

1. *Preheat the oven and prepare the muffin tin.* Preheat the oven to 350°F. Line 2 wells of the muffin tin with paper cupcake liners.

2. *Make the cupcake batter.* In a small bowl, whisk together the flour, baking powder, and salt. In a medium bowl, using an electric mixer on medium-high, cream the butter and granulated sugar until light and fluffy, about 3 minutes. Add the vanilla extract and egg white and beat to incorporate. Add the champagne, orange zest, and orange juice and beat again to incorporate. Add the flour mixture and beat until just incorporated.

3. ***Bake the cupcakes.*** Divide the batter between the lined wells, making sure not to fill each more than two-thirds full. Bake for about 20 minutes, until a toothpick inserted into the center comes out clean. Let cool in pan for a minute or two, then transfer the cupcakes in their liners to a wire rack to cool completely.

4. ***Make the frosting.*** In a medium bowl, cream together the butter, confectioners' sugar, champagne, orange zest, orange juice, and salt until the mixture is well combined and thick.

5. ***Decorate the cupcakes.*** Once the cupcakes are completely cooled, pipe or spread on the frosting. Serve.

## *Tip*

If you want even more intense champagne flavor, add a drop or two of champagne-flavored oil, which you can find online, at cake-decorating shops, or in the cake-decorating section of a craft store like Michael's or Jo-Ann.

# Mini Pumpkin Cheesecakes

**Makes 2 mini cheesecakes • Prep time: 10 minutes • Cook time: 24 to 26 minutes**

If you love pumpkin pie and you love cheesecake, this dessert is bound to knock your socks off. Creamy, dense cheesecake flavored with puréed pumpkin and pumpkin pie spice sits atop a crunchy gingersnap-crumb crust. This recipe makes two individual-size cheesecakes, so you can eat the whole thing without regret.

**FOR THE CRUST**

3 tablespoons gingersnap crumbs (from about 4 cookies)
3 tablespoons light brown sugar
1½ tablespoons unsalted butter, melted

**FOR THE FILLING**

¼ cup pumpkin purée
1 large egg
3 tablespoons light brown sugar
¾ teaspoon pumpkin pie spice
Pinch kosher salt

4 ounces cream cheese, at room temperature
3 tablespoons granulated sugar
¼ teaspoon vanilla

1. **Preheat the oven and make the crust.** Preheat the oven to 350°F. In a small bowl, combine the gingersnap crumbs, brown sugar, and melted butter, and stir to mix well. Press the mixture firmly into the bottom of the ramekins. Refrigerate while you make the filling.

2. **Make the filling.** In a medium bowl, combine the pumpkin purée, egg, brown sugar, pumpkin pie spice, and salt. Mix well. In a separate medium bowl, combine the cream cheese, granulated sugar, and vanilla and mix until well combined and creamy. Add the pumpkin mixture to the cream cheese mixture and stir until smooth and combined.

3. **Bake the cheesecakes.** Divide the filling between the crusts. Bake for 24 to 26 minutes, until the centers are set. Let cool to room temperature. Cover with plastic wrap and refrigerate for at least 2 hours before serving.

## Tip

Make these mini cheesecakes even more special by topping them with a dollop of lightly sweetened whipped cream with a dash of pumpkin pie spice or cinnamon mixed in.

# No-Bake Tiramisu Cheesecakes

EQUIPMENT/TOOLS: TWO 6-OUNCE RAMEKINS, ELECTRIC MIXER, PLASTIC WRAP

**Makes 2 mini cheesecakes • Prep time: 15 minutes, plus 4 hours to chill • No-Bake**

These mini cheesecakes marry all the things we love about tiramisu—the luscious Italian dessert that layers coffee-soaked ladyfingers, creamy mascarpone cheese, and cocoa powder—with all the things we love about cheesecake—a crunchy cookie-crumb crust and a rich, dense filling.

### FOR THE CRUST
½ cup vanilla wafer crumbs

1½ tablespoons unsalted butter, melted

### FOR THE FILLING
3 ounces cream cheese, at room temperature

2 ounces mascarpone cheese, at room temperature

3 tablespoons granulated sugar, divided

2 tablespoons plus 2 teaspoons heavy (whipping) cream

¼ teaspoon vanilla extract

### FOR THE COFFEE-SOAKED LADYFINGERS
¼ cup warm water

2 tablespoons instant espresso powder

1 teaspoon granulated sugar

4 ladyfingers

### FOR THE TOPPING
1 tablespoon unsweetened cocoa powder

1. **Make the crust.** In a small bowl, stir together the cookie crumbs and melted butter. Press the mixture into the bottom of your cooking vessels. Chill for 20 minutes while you make the filling.

2. **Make the filling.** In a medium bowl, combine the cream cheese, mascarpone cheese, and 2 tablespoons of sugar using the electric mixer on medium-high. In a separate bowl, using the mixer or a whisk, combine the cream, vanilla, and the remaining tablespoon of sugar. Whip until stiff peaks form. Using a rubber spatula, gently fold the whipped cream into the cheese mixture.

3. **Make the coffee-soaked ladyfingers.** In a small bowl, combine the warm water, espresso powder, and sugar and stir to mix well. Submerge the ladyfingers into the coffee mixture, one at a time, then place two in each vessel on top of the crust.

➤

**4.** ***Assemble the cheesecakes.*** Spread the filling evenly over the ladyfingers. Cover with plastic wrap and chill in the refrigerator for at least 4 hours or overnight. To serve, run a knife around the inside of the ramekins to loosen the cheesecake and then carefully invert onto a plate. Invert again so that the crust is on the bottom. Sift the cocoa powder over the tops of the cheesecakes and serve.

## Equipment Hack

Use two widemouthed 8-ounce canning jars instead.

## Tip

Instead of the cocoa powder, you can top these little cheesecakes with whipped cream spiked with a bit of Kahlúa or other coffee liqueur.

# Coffee Crumb Cake

**Makes 2 pieces • Prep time: 10 minutes • Cook time: 22 to 24 minutes • Mini Equipment**

Coffee-flavored cake with a crumb topping (a surprise ribbon of which is hidden in the center of the cake) makes a fantastic dessert. But because it's technically a coffee cake, you can totally justify eating it for breakfast. Or enjoy during an afternoon break. Or a late-night treat. Or . . .

**FOR THE TOPPING**

¼ cup light brown sugar

1 tablespoon granulated sugar

Pinch kosher salt

¼ teaspoon cinnamon

1 tablespoon unsalted
   butter, melted

3 tablespoons all-purpose flour

**FOR THE CAKE**

¼ cup vegetable oil

⅓ cup granulated sugar

Pinch kosher salt

1 large egg

2 tablespoons sour cream

2 tablespoons strong brewed
   coffee, at room temperature

¼ teaspoon vanilla extract

1/3 cup plus 1 tablespoon
   all-purpose flour

⅛ teaspoon baking powder

⅛ teaspoon baking soda

1. ***Preheat the oven and prepare the pan.*** Preheat the oven to 375°F. Grease your cooking vessel(s) with baking spray.

2. ***Make the topping.*** In a small bowl, stir together the brown sugar, granulated sugar, salt, cinnamon, melted butter, and flour and mix until it clumps.

3. ***Make the cake batter.*** In a medium bowl, using an electric mixer on medium-high, cream the oil and sugar together for about 3 minutes. Add the salt, egg, sour cream, coffee, and vanilla and beat to combine. Add the flour, baking powder, and baking soda and beat until just incorporated.

**4. *Bake the cake.*** Transfer half the batter to the prepared vessel(s). Sprinkle half the topping mixture over the batter, then top with the remaining batter and the remaining topping mixture. Bake for 22 to 24 minutes, until the cake is golden brown on top and a toothpick inserted into the center comes out clean. Let cool in the pan on a wire rack. Serve warm or at room temperature.

## Equipment Hack

Use two 8-ounce ramekins instead.

## Tip

If you don't have a mini loaf pan, you can make muffins instead. The recipe will make 4 standard-size muffins. They may cook a bit faster, so check them after 20 minutes in the oven.

# Blueberry Yogurt Cake

**Makes 4 slices • Prep time: 10 minutes • Cook time: 1 hour • Lightly Sweet**

If you've ever been tempted to eat cake for breakfast, this one was practically made for it. It's loaded with blueberries, and it's got yogurt in it, so it's pretty much a yogurt parfait in cake form.

2 tablespoons plus
 2 teaspoons plain
 whole-milk yogurt

1 large egg

½ teaspoon finely grated
 lemon zest

¼ teaspoon vanilla extract

4 tablespoons granulated
 sugar, divided

¾ teaspoon baking powder

⅛ teaspoon kosher salt

½ cup plus 1 teaspoon
 all-purpose flour, divided

2 tablespoons plus
 2 teaspoons vegetable oil

1 cup frozen blueberries

1. ***Preheat the oven and prepare the pan.*** Preheat the oven to 350°F. Grease your cooking vessel(s) with baking spray.

2. ***Make the batter.*** In a medium bowl, whisk the yogurt, egg, lemon zest, vanilla, and 3 tablespoons of sugar until smooth. Add the baking powder, salt, and ½ cup of flour and whisk to combine. Add the oil and whisk until well incorporated. In a small bowl, toss the blueberries with the remaining teaspoon of flour to coat. Using a rubber spatula, gently fold the blueberries into the batter.

3. ***Bake the cake.*** Transfer the batter to the prepared pan. Sprinkle the remaining tablespoon of sugar over the top. Bake for about 1 hour, until the top is golden brown and a toothpick inserted into the center comes out clean. Let the cake cool in the pan for about 10 minutes. Remove the cake from the pan and let cool completely on a wire rack.

## Equipment Hack

Use two 8-ounce ramekins instead.

## Tip

For even more blueberry flavor, you can substitute blueberry yogurt for the plain yogurt. This will also make the cake a bit sweeter.

# Mini Pineapple Upside-Down Cakes

EQUIPMENT/TOOLS: TWO 6-OUNCE RAMEKINS, BAKING SPRAY,
ELECTRIC MIXER, WIRE RACK

**Makes 2 cakes • Prep time: 10 minutes • Cook time: 20 to 24 minutes**

Besides being adorable, these mini cakes are incredibly delicious. The cake is just a basic white cake, but the caramelized pineapple topping is both beautiful and intensely flavorful. The cherry is optional, but adds a cute splash of color and a bright pop of flavor.

**FOR THE TOPPING**

1 tablespoon butter, melted

2 tablespoons light brown sugar

2 pineapple rings, fresh or canned

2 maraschino cherries (optional)

**FOR THE CAKE**

¼ cup all-purpose flour

¼ teaspoon baking powder

Pinch kosher salt

1 tablespoon unsalted butter, at room temperature

1 tablespoon plus 1 teaspoon light brown sugar

1 tablespoon plus 1 teaspoon granulated sugar

1 large egg white

¼ teaspoon vanilla extract

2 tablespoons whole milk

1. **Preheat the oven and prepare the ramekins.** Preheat oven to 350°F. Grease your ramekins with baking spray.

2. **Make the topping.** In a small bowl, stir the butter and brown sugar together until creamy. Divide the mixture evenly between the two prepared ramekins. Place one pineapple ring in the bottom of each ramekin (trim to fit if necessary), and then place 1 cherry (if using) in the middle of each ring.

3. **Make the cake batter.** In a small bowl, whisk together the flour, baking powder, and salt. In a medium bowl, using an electric mixer on medium-high, cream together the butter, brown sugar, and granulated sugar until light and fluffy, about 3 minutes. Add the egg white and vanilla and mix to combine. Add the dry ingredients and the milk, and mix until just combined. Divide the batter between the ramekins.

4. **Bake the cakes.** Bake for 20 to 24 minutes, until a toothpick inserted into the center comes out clean. Let cool on a wire rack for 10 minutes. Run a knife around the inside of each ramekin to loosen the cakes and then invert them onto plates. Let cool to room temperature and serve.

# *Mini Carrot Cakes*

**EQUIPMENT/TOOLS: 8-INCH SQUARE BAKING PAN, PARCHMENT PAPER, BAKING SPRAY, ELECTRIC MIXER, WIRE RACK, 2½-INCH ROUND COOKIE/BISCUIT CUTTER**

**Makes 2 cakes • Prep time: 20 minutes • Cook time: 20 minutes**

With layers of moist, spicy carrot cake covered with a decadent cream cheese frosting, these individual mini cakes are perfect for a special occasion—especially around the spring holidays. You'll end up with some extra cake, which you can crumble and mix with any leftover frosting to make cake balls. Coat the cake balls with melted white chocolate or make them egg shaped and use pastel-colored candy melts for the coating.

**FOR THE CAKE**

1 cup plus 1 tablespoon
   all-purpose flour

1 teaspoon baking powder

¾ teaspoon ground cinnamon

¼ teaspoon ground nutmeg

¼ teaspoon baking soda

¼ teaspoon kosher salt

⅔ cup grated fresh carrots

½ cup freshly squeezed
   orange juice

¼ cup plus 1½ tablespoons
   granulated sugar

2½ tablespoons vegetable oil

1 large egg white

¾ teaspoon vanilla extract

**FOR THE FROSTING**

4 ounces cream cheese,
   at room temperature

2½ tablespoons unsalted
   butter, at room temperature

½ teaspoon vanilla extract

1 cup confectioners' sugar

1. ***Preheat the oven and prepare the pan.*** Preheat the oven to 375°F. Line the square baking pan with parchment paper so that the paper hangs over the sides. Grease the pan and the paper with baking spray.

2. ***Make the cake batter.*** In a medium bowl, whisk together the flour, baking powder, cinnamon, nutmeg, baking soda, and salt. In another medium bowl, combine the carrots, orange juice, sugar, oil, egg white, and vanilla and stir to mix well. Add the wet ingredients to the dry ingredients and stir until incorporated.

3. ***Bake the cake.*** Pour the batter into the prepared pan and spread into an even layer. Bake for about 20 minutes, until a toothpick inserted into the center comes out clean. Set the pan on a wire rack to cool for 10 to 15 minutes. Use the parchment paper overhang to lift the cake from the pan onto the wire rack to cool completely.

➤

4. ***Make the frosting.*** In a medium bowl, using an electric mixer on medium-high or a whisk, beat the cream cheese, butter, and vanilla together until creamy, about 2 minutes. Add the confectioners' sugar and continue to beat until fluffy.

5. ***Assemble and frost the cakes.*** Transfer the cooled cake to a cutting board. Using a round cookie or biscuit cutter, cut out four rounds. Spread the frosting over the top of two of the rounds, then top with the other two rounds. Spread the remaining frosting over the tops and sides of the cakes. Serve.

## Equipment Hack

Use four 8-ounce ramekins instead.

## Tip

For extra flavor and texture, add a couple of tablespoons of sweetened shredded coconut, raisins, and/or pecans to the cake batter.

# Mini Confetti Cakes

**Makes 2 mini cakes • Prep time: 15 minutes • Cook time: 16 to 18 minutes**

Confetti is the perfect thing to mark a celebration, but it's even better when it's edible and mixed into a perfect individual-size cake. If you don't have buttermilk, you can substitute plain yogurt or use regular milk combined with 1½ teaspoons of lemon juice. Let the milk mixture stand for a few minutes before adding.

### FOR THE CAKE

1⅓ cups all-purpose flour

½ teaspoon baking powder

¼ teaspoon kosher salt

⅔ cup granulated sugar

1 teaspoon grated lemon zest

½ cup (1 stick) plus
  2½ tablespoons butter, at
  room temperature

1 large egg

2 teaspoons freshly squeezed
  lemon juice

½ cup plus
  1½ tablespoons buttermilk

3 tablespoons
  rainbow sprinkles

### FOR THE GLAZE

2½ tablespoons
  confectioners' sugar

1½ tablespoons freshly
  squeezed lemon juice

1 tablespoon rainbow sprinkles

1. ***Preheat the oven and prepare the pan.*** Preheat the oven to 350°F. Grease your cooking vessels with baking spray.

2. ***Make the batter.*** In a medium bowl, whisk together the flour, baking powder, and salt. In another medium bowl, whisk together the sugar and lemon zest. Add the butter and use an electric mixer on medium-high to cream it with the sugar until it is pale and fluffy, about 3 minutes. Add the egg and the lemon juice and beat until just incorporated. Add half of the flour mixture and beat until just incorporated. Add the buttermilk and beat to combine. Beat in the remaining flour until just incorporated. Using a rubber spatula, gently fold in the sprinkles.

3. ***Bake the cakes.*** Divide the cake batter between the two prepared vessels. Bake for 16 to 18 minutes, until a toothpick inserted into the center comes out clean. Let the cakes cool in their pans for 10 to 15 minutes on a wire rack. Invert the cakes onto the rack and cool completely.

4. ***Make the glaze.*** In a small bowl, whisk together the confectioners' sugar and lemon juice until well combined. Drizzle the glaze over the cooled cakes. Garnish with the sprinkles and serve.

# Molten Lava Cakes

EQUIPMENT/TOOLS: TWO 6-OUNCE RAMEKINS, BAKING SHEET

**Makes 2 cakes • Prep time: 10 minutes • Cook time: 12 to 14 minutes • Quick**

These rich little cakes that ooze chocolate from their centers when you cut into them seem like restaurant-level culinary magic. But they're actually super easy to make. They make the perfect dessert for a romantic dinner for two, or you can easily scale up the recipe for a dinner party.

3 tablespoons unsalted butter, plus additional for greasing the ramekins

3 tablespoons plus 2 teaspoons granulated sugar, divided

3 ounces bittersweet chocolate, finely chopped

1 large egg plus 1 large egg yolk

¼ teaspoon vanilla extract

⅛ teaspoon kosher salt

3 tablespoons all-purpose flour

Confectioners' sugar, for garnish

Raspberries, for garnish (optional)

1. **Preheat the oven and prepare the ramekins.** Preheat the oven to 400°F. Grease your cooking vessels with butter. Put 1 teaspoon of the sugar in each ramekin and shake it around to coat the bottom and sides. Shake out the excess sugar. Place the ramekins on a baking sheet.

2. **Melt the chocolate.** In a microwave-safe bowl, combine the chocolate and remaining 3 tablespoons of butter. Heat in 30-second intervals in the microwave, stirring in between, until the chocolate is fully melted and the mixture is smooth.

3. **Make the batter.** In a medium bowl, whisk together the egg, egg yolk, the remaining 3 tablespoons of sugar, vanilla, and salt. Stir in the melted chocolate, then stir in the flour until just incorporated.

4. **Bake the cakes.** Divide the batter between the prepared vessels. Bake for 12 to 14 minutes, until the top is dry. Let cool for about 2 minutes before running a knife around the inside of the ramekins to loosen the cakes from the sides. Carefully invert the cakes onto dessert plates. Garnish with confectioners' sugar and raspberries (if using).

## Tip

For extra insurance that the cakes will slide out of the ramekins easily, you can line the bottoms of the ramekins with rounds of parchment paper sprayed with baking spray and skip dusting with sugar.

# Chocolate-Hazelnut Mug Cakes

**Makes 2 mug cakes • Prep time: 5 minutes • Cook time: 1 to 2 minutes • Quick**

Microwavable mug cakes are the absolute best things for dessert emergencies. They are quick and easy to make, use pantry staples, and are totally satisfying. A dollop of whipped cream or a scoop of vanilla ice cream on top certainly wouldn't hurt, but these chocolaty cakes are perfectly rich and delicious on their own. Dessert emergency averted.

¼ cup chocolate-hazelnut spread (such as Nutella)

¼ cup all-purpose flour

1 tablespoon granulated sugar

2 teaspoons unsweetened cocoa powder

1 teaspoon baking powder

2 large eggs

1 teaspoon vanilla extract

¼ cup semisweet chocolate chips

1. **Melt the spread.** Place the chocolate-hazelnut spread in a medium microwave-safe bowl and heat in the microwave for 20 seconds.

2. **Make the batter.** Add the flour, sugar, cocoa powder, baking powder, eggs, and vanilla to the bowl and mix well. Stir in the chocolate chips.

3. **Bake the cake.** Divide the batter between the two cooking vessels. Microwave on high until the cake rises and the middle sets, 1 to 2 minutes. Let stand for 1 to 2 minutes before serving.

## Equipment Hack

Use two widemouthed canning jars instead.

## Tip

If you don't have chocolate-hazelnut spread, you can substitute another nut butter (peanut, almond, etc.). If so, reduce the amount to 3 tablespoons.

# Red Velvet Mug Cakes

**Makes 2 mug cakes • Prep time: 5 minutes • Cook time: 1 minute • Quick**

Red velvet is a classic cake characterized by a rich cocoa flavor, the tang of buttermilk, and a distinctive red crumb (thanks, usually, to food coloring). This version is super quick and you can make just 1 serving or several, depending on the moment.

¼ cup plus 2 tablespoons milk

1 teaspoon white vinegar

½ cup all-purpose flour

½ cup granulated sugar

2 tablespoons unsweetened cocoa powder

¼ teaspoon baking powder

⅛ teaspoon kosher salt

¼ cup plus 2 tablespoons vegetable oil

1 drop red gel food coloring (optional)

1. **Sour the milk.** In a medium bowl, whisk the milk and vinegar together and let stand for a few minutes.

2. **Make the batter.** Add the flour, sugar, cocoa powder, baking powder, and salt to the milk mixture and stir to mix well. Add the vegetable oil and food coloring (if using) and mix until smooth.

3. **Microwave the cake.** Divide the batter between the cooking vessels. Microwave on high for 45 seconds. The cake should puff up when cooked through. Cook for an additional 15 to 30 seconds, if needed. Serve immediately.

## Equipment Hack

Use two widemouthed canning jars instead.

## Tip

If you happen to have buttermilk or sour cream on hand, use ¼ cup plus 2 tablespoons of that in place of the milk and white vinegar. To incorporate the flavor of a cream cheese frosting, stir 2 tablespoons of room temperature cream cheese with 2 teaspoons of sugar and drop half into each mug of batter before microwaving.

# *Peanut Butter Banana Cakes*

**EQUIPMENT/TOOLS: TWO 6-OUNCE RAMEKINS, BAKING SPRAY**

**Makes 2 cakes • Prep time: 5 minutes • Cook time: 12 to 14 minutes • Quick**

I have been known to resort to peanut butter and bananas on toast when my sweet tooth comes in and I'm looking for a quick fix. These cakes are almost as easy and so much yummier! If you've got chocolate chips, add a tablespoon or so to the batter in each jar before baking.

½ cup all-purpose flour
½ cup granulated sugar
1 teaspoon baking powder
2 large eggs

¼ cup plus 2 tablespoons
    creamy peanut butter
¼ cup plus 2 tablespoons milk

¼ cup plus 2 tablespoons
    vegetable oil
2 bananas, sliced

1. ***Preheat the oven and prepare the ramekins.*** Preheat the oven to 350°F. Grease your cooking vessels with baking spray.

2. ***Make the batter.*** In a medium bowl, whisk together the flour, sugar, baking powder, eggs, peanut butter, milk, and oil until smooth. Stir in the banana slices.

3. ***Bake the cake.*** Divide the mixture between the prepared ramekins. Bake for 12 to 14 minutes, until a toothpick inserted into the center comes out clean. Serve warm.

## *Equipment Hack*

Use two large oven-safe coffee mugs instead.

## *Tip*

Need it even faster? These can be made even quicker in the microwave. Heat for 60 to 90 seconds, until a toothpick inserted into the center comes out clean.

# S'mores Cakes

**Makes 2 cakes** • **Prep time: 5 minutes** • **Cook time: 37 minutes**

S'mores are a classic campfire treat, but this recipe brings them inside. These cakes have all the elements of classic s'mores—graham crackers, melty chocolate, and toasted marshmallows—but the magic takes place in the oven.

**FOR THE CRUST**

2 whole graham cracker sheets, broken into pieces

1½ tablespoons granulated sugar

2 tablespoons unsalted butter, melted

**FOR THE CAKE**

¼ cup all-purpose flour

3 tablespoons unsweetened cocoa powder

½ teaspoon baking powder

Pinch kosher salt

2 tablespoons unsalted butter, at room temperature

¼ cup granulated sugar

1 large egg

½ teaspoon vanilla extract

2 tablespoons heavy (whipping) cream

2 tablespoons mini semisweet chocolate chips

8 large marshmallows

1. ***Preheat the oven and prepare the ramekins.*** Preheat the oven to 350°F. Coat the insides of two ramekins with baking spray and place them on a baking sheet.

2. ***Make the crust.*** Pulse the graham crackers in a food processor to turn them into crumbs. Add the sugar and butter and pulse to combine. The mixture should be the texture of wet sand. Divide the mixture between the two ramekins and press it into the bottoms and up the sides. Bake for about 12 minutes, until the crust puffs up and begins to brown.

3. ***Make the cake batter.*** In a small bowl, whisk together the flour, cocoa powder, baking powder, and salt. In a medium bowl, use an electric mixer on medium-high to cream together the butter and sugar until fluffy, about 3 minutes. Add the egg and vanilla and beat to incorporate. Add half the flour mixture and all of the cream and beat to incorporate. Add the remaining flour and beat until just incorporated. Using a spoon or rubber spatula, fold in the chocolate chips.

4. ***Bake the cake.*** Divide the batter between the ramekins. Bake for about 20 minutes, until a toothpick inserted into the center comes out clean. Remove the pan from the oven and raise the temperature to 500°F.

5. ***Toast the marshmallows.*** Press 4 marshmallows onto the top of each cake. Return the pan to the oven and bake for about 5 minutes, until the marshmallows are soft and lightly toasted. Let cool for a minute or two before serving. Serve warm.

## *Tip*

For a bit of a flavor twist, use cinnamon graham crackers in place of plain ones.

# Graham Cracker Lime Icebox Cake

EQUIPMENT/TOOLS: SAUCEPAN, BAKING SHEET, PLASTIC WRAP

**Makes 2 pieces • Prep time: 10 minutes, plus 7 hours to chill • Cook time: 5 minutes • No-Bake**

Icebox cakes are delightfully easy to make. The basic idea supports all sorts of flavor combinations. This version is tart and sweet, and, served chilled, this is an ideal summer dessert.

**FOR THE FILLING**

3 tablespoons
   granulated sugar
1 tablespoon cornstarch
Pinch kosher salt
1 large egg yolk

½ cup heavy (whipping) cream
1 tablespoon unsalted butter
Zest of 1 lime
Juice of 1 lime

**FOR THE CAKES**

10 graham cracker squares

**FOR THE WHIPPED CREAM**

¼ cup heavy (whipping) cream
1 tablespoon
   confectioners' sugar

1. ***Make the filling.*** In a small saucepan over medium heat, whisk together the sugar, cornstarch, and salt. Whisk in the egg yolk and ½ cup of cream and cook, whisking constantly, until it comes to a boil. Continue cooking, whisking constantly, for another minute, until the mixture thickens. Remove the pan from the heat and add the butter and lime zest. Whisk until the butter is melted and incorporated. Whisk in the lime juice. Set aside to cool for about 10 minutes.

2. ***Assemble the cakes.*** Place two graham cracker squares on a baking sheet or platter with space in between them. Spread one-quarter of the filling onto the graham crackers. Place the next two graham cracker squares on top of the first two and repeat this three more times, ending with the last two graham cracker squares on top. Cover loosely with plastic wrap and chill in the refrigerator for at least 6 hours.

3. ***Top with whipped cream.*** Using an electric mixer on medium-high, beat the ¼ cup of cream with the confectioners' sugar until it forms soft peaks. Unwrap the stacks and spread the whipped cream all over the top and sides. Refrigerate for 1 hour before serving.

## *Tip*

To give this cake a tropical twist, top each stack with a tablespoon of toasted sweetened shredded coconut.

# Lemon Pudding Cakes

**Makes 2 cakes • Prep time: 10 minutes • Cook time: 30 minutes**

These bright, delicate, and lemony cakes are two desserts in one. The mixture magically separates into two layers as it bakes—a rich, creamy pudding layer with a fluffy cake layer on top. Serve these as is or garnished with confectioners' sugar, whipped cream, or fresh berries.

| | | |
|---|---|---|
| Butter, at room temperature, for preparing the ramekins | 3 tablespoons granulated sugar | 3 tablespoons all-purpose flour |
| 1 large egg, at room temperature, yolk and white separated | 2 tablespoons unsalted butter, melted | 1 teaspoon grated lemon zest |
| | ¼ teaspoon vanilla extract | 1 tablespoon freshly squeezed lemon juice |
| | | ½ cup milk, slightly warm |

1. **Preheat the oven and prepare the ramekins.** Preheat the oven to 325°F. Grease your cooking vessels with the room-temperature butter.

2. **Make the batter.** In a medium bowl, use an electric mixer on high to whip the egg white to stiff peaks. In another medium bowl, whisk the egg yolk and sugar together until the mixture becomes pale. Add the melted butter and vanilla and beat to incorporate. Add the flour and beat again to fully incorporate. Whisk in the lemon zest and juice. Whisk in the milk. Using a rubber spatula, gently fold the whipped egg white until just barely incorporated.

3. **Bake the cakes.** Divide the batter between the cooking vessels. Bake for about 30 minutes, until the top is firm to the touch. Let the cakes cool completely before serving.

## Tip

You can substitute any citrus you like—orange, blood orange, lime, or grapefruit—for the lemon. Or try a combination.

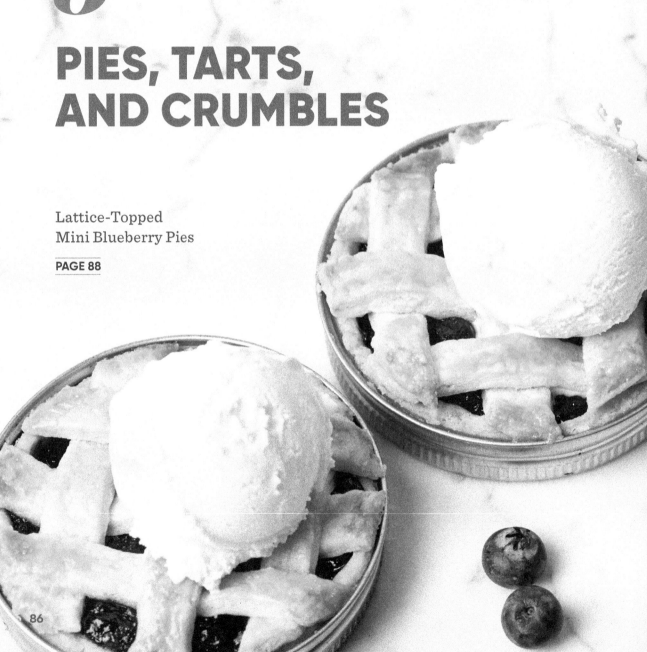

# 5

# PIES, TARTS,
AND CRUMBLES

Lattice-Topped
Mini Blueberry Pies

**PAGE 88**

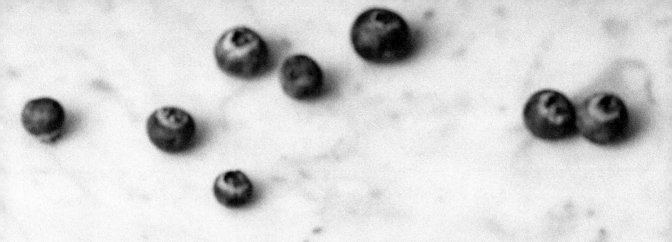

*T*iny pies, hand pies, mini tarts, and individual-size crisps, cobblers, and crumbles win high praise. They look adorable and taste even better. From toy-size yet big-flavored Lattice-Topped Mini Blueberry Pies to Strawberry and Dark Chocolate Hand Pies, and the Mixed Berry and Pastry Cream Tartlet to Brown Sugar Cinnamon Stuffed Apple Crisp, these individual filled pastries always delight.

Lattice-Topped Mini Blueberry Pies **88**

Sour Cream Apple Mini Pies **90**

Banana Cream Mini Pies **92**

Lemon Meringue Mini Pies **94**

Pumpkin Mini Pies **96**

Bourbon Pecan Pie **97**

Chocolate Mousse Pie **99**

Peach Hand Pies **101**

Strawberry and Dark Chocolate Hand Pies **103**

No-Bake Key Lime Pie Cups **105**

Cinnamon Pear Galettes **106**

Fig, Honey, and Blue Cheese Galettes **107**

Lemon Curd Tarts **109**

Raspberry Jam–Filled Mini Tartlets **110**

Mixed Berry and Pastry Cream Tartlet **112**

Dark Chocolate Cherry Tartlet **114**

Brown Sugar Cinnamon Stuffed Apple Crisp **115**

Pear and Coconut Crisp **116**

Blackberry Cobbler **117**

Bourbon Peach Cobbler **118**

Strawberry Rhubarb Crumble **119**

# Lattice-Topped Mini Blueberry Pies

**EQUIPMENT/TOOLS: PATRY CUTTER, PLASTIC WRAP, SAUCEPAN, ROLLING PIN, MINI PIE PAN**

**Makes 2 mini pies • Prep time: 20 minutes, plus 30 minutes to chill • Cook time: 40 minutes**

A 6-inch blueberry pie with a lattice-woven pastry crust top is as tasty as it is adorable. In fact, you might want to double up this recipe and stash one of the pies (unbaked) in the freezer for the next time you want an amazing dessert without the hassle. You can substitute other berries, like blackberries or strawberries, for the blueberries.

**FOR THE CRUST**

1¼ cups all-purpose flour, plus additional for dusting

1 teaspoon granulated sugar

½ teaspoon kosher salt

½ cup (1 stick) cold unsalted butter, cut into small pieces

2 to 3 tablespoons ice water

1 large egg whisked with 1 teaspoon water

**FOR THE FILLING**

½ cup fresh or frozen blueberries

1½ teaspoons brown sugar

1 tablespoon granulated sugar

½ teaspoon cornstarch

⅛ teaspoon cinnamon

1. **Make the crust.** In a medium bowl, whisk together the flour, sugar, and salt. Add the butter and using a pastry cutter, fork, or two knives, cut the butter into the flour mixture until there are pea-size clumps of dough. Sprinkle 2 tablespoons of water over the dough and mix until the dough comes together in a ball. If it is still crumbly, add more water, 1 teaspoon at a time until the dough comes together. Flatten the ball into a disk shape and then wrap it tightly in plastic wrap. Chill in the refrigerator for at least 30 minutes.

2. **Preheat the oven and make the filling.** Preheat the oven to 375°F. In a small saucepan over medium heat, stir together the berries, brown sugar, granulated sugar, cornstarch, and cinnamon. Cook, stirring occasionally, until the berries soften and the sugar dissolves. Use the back of the spoon to crush some of the berries. Remove the pan from the heat and let cool.

3. **Assemble the crust.** Split the dough into two pieces, one slightly larger than the other. If using canning jar lids, split the dough into four pieces. On a lightly floured surface, roll out the larger piece into an 8- to 9-inch round, about ¼-inch thick. Place this round into a mini pie dish, pressing the dough into the bottom and trimming any overhang around the edges. Prick the bottom several times with a fork or add pie weights. Bake for about 10 minutes. Let the crust cool and remove the pie weights. Meanwhile, roll the smaller dough piece into a 6- to 7-inch round, also ¼-inch thick. Cut the round into strips ½- to 1-inch wide.

4. **Assemble the pie.** Add the filling to the par-baked crust. Lay the dough strips on top, alternating the strips over and under each other for a latticed look. Trim any excess dough and crimp the dough strips and the edge of the bottom dough together. Brush the dough with the egg wash.

5. **Bake the pie.** Bake 25 to 30 minutes or until the crust is lightly browned. Cool slightly before serving.

## Equipment Hack

Use two widemouthed metal canning jar lids instead.

## Tip

You can make the dough in a food processor to save time. Put the flour and salt in the processor. Add the butter and pulse until pea-size dough clumps form. Add 2 tablespoons of ice water and process just until the dough comes together in a ball. If it is too dry, add additional water, 1 teaspoon at a time.

# Sour Cream Apple Mini Pies

EQUIPMENT/TOOLS: PASTRY CUTTER, PLASTIC WRAP, ROLLING PIN, WIDEMOUTHED METAL CANNING JAR LIDS, WIRE RACK

**Makes 2 mini pies** • **Prep time: 20 minutes, plus 30 minutes to chill dough** • **Cook time: 25 to 30 minutes**

Apple pie is an American classic. This version includes sour cream in the filling for added richness. You can use whatever baking apples you like here. I like a tart-sweet, crisp apple like Granny Smith or Fuji. A scoop of Easy No-Churn Vanilla Ice Cream (page 166) or store-bought ice cream takes it over the top.

**FOR THE CRUST**

½ cup plus 2 tablespoons all-purpose flour, plus additional for dusting

½ teaspoon sugar

¼ teaspoon kosher salt

¼ cup cold unsalted butter, cut into small pieces

1½ to 2 tablespoons ice water

**FOR THE FILLING**

¼ cup sour cream

3 tablespoons brown sugar

1½ teaspoons all-purpose flour

¼ teaspoon vanilla extract

Pinch kosher salt

¾ cup chopped apple (about 1 large apple, peeled and cored)

**FOR THE TOPPING**

2 tablespoons all-purpose flour

1½ tablespoons brown sugar

1 tablespoon unsalted butter, at room temperature

1. ***Make the crust.*** In a medium bowl, whisk together the flour, sugar, and salt. Add the butter. Using a pastry cutter, fork, or two knives, cut the butter into the flour mixture until there are pea-size clumps of dough. Sprinkle 1½ tablespoons of water over the dough and mix until the dough comes together in a ball. If the dough is dry, add additional water, ½ teaspoon at a time, until the dough comes together. Flatten the ball into a disk shape and wrap it tightly in plastic wrap. Chill in the refrigerator for 30 minutes.

2. ***Preheat the oven and make the filling.*** Preheat the oven to 375°F. In a medium bowl, stir together the sour cream, brown sugar, flour, vanilla, and salt. Add the apple and mix to coat.

3. ***Make the topping.*** In a small bowl, add the flour, brown sugar, and butter and mix with a fork to form a crumbly mixture.

4. **Assemble the pies.** On a lightly floured surface, roll out the dough into a round about ¼-inch thick. Using your vessel of choice as a guide, cut out two circles about ½ inch wider than the ring. If using metal canning jar lids, place the lid tops into the rings with the rubber side down (so that you are cooking on the metal side). Press the pastry circles into the lids. Divide the filling between the piecrusts. Spoon the topping mixture over the filling.

5. **Bake the pies.** Bake for 25 to 30 minutes, until the tops are lightly browned and the filling is bubbling. Let cool on a wire rack before serving warm or at room temperature. To serve, run a knife around the inside of the rings and lift the pies out.

## Equipment Hack

Use two ramekins instead.

## Tip

Sometimes you just don't have the time to make your own pastry dough. You can use one round from a package of refrigerated pie dough from the supermarket.

# *Banana Cream Mini Pies*

EQUIPMENT/TOOLS: FOOD PROCESSOR, MINI PIE DISH, SAUCEPAN,
FINE-MESH STRAINER, PLASTIC WRAP, ELECTRIC MIXER

**Makes 2 mini pies** • **Prep time: 20 minutes, plus 1 hour to chill** •
**Cook time: 10 minutes** • **Mini Equipment**

Cream pies are my favorite. I just can't get enough of a rich, custardy filling in a flaky pastry crust. Bananas give this one plenty of flavor without making it too sweet. Sometimes I'll add a layer of caramel sauce or chocolate ganache on top of the crust for a sweet surprise.

**FOR THE CRUST**

6 graham crackers

2 tablespoons sugar

2 tablespoons unsalted
   butter, melted

**FOR THE FILLING**

1 cup milk

½ teaspoon vanilla extract

¼ cup plus
   2 tablespoons sugar

3 tablespoons cornstarch

3 large egg yolks

1 tablespoon unsalted butter

2 bananas, sliced

**FOR THE TOPPING**

1 cup heavy
   (whipping) cream

1 tablespoon
   confectioners' sugar

½ teaspoon vanilla extract

1. ***Preheat the oven and make the crust.*** Preheat the oven to 350°F. In a food processor, pulse the graham crackers with the sugar until they become coarse crumbs. Add the butter and pulse to incorporate. The mixture should be the texture of wet sand. Press the crumb mixture into the bottom of the vessel of your choice in an even layer, ¼- to ½-inch thick. Bake for about 10 minutes, until the crust just begins to brown.

2. ***Make the filling.*** In a small saucepan over medium heat, bring the milk to a simmer. Remove the pan from the heat and stir in the vanilla. In a medium bowl, using an electric mixer on medium, a whisk, or a spoon, beat together the sugar, cornstarch, and egg yolks until the mixture lightens in color, about 1 minute. Whisk about ⅓ of the warm milk into the egg yolk mixture to temper it, then pour the egg yolk mixture into the remaining milk. Set the pan over medium heat. Cook, stirring constantly, just until the mixture comes to a boil, then remove the pan from the heat. Add the butter and stir until it is completely melted and incorporated. Using a fine-mesh strainer, strain this mixture into a bowl. Cover the bowl with plastic, pressing it onto the surface of the mixture, and refrigerate for at least 1 hour.

3. ***Make the topping.*** In a medium bowl, use an electric mixer on medium-high to whip the cream, sugar, and vanilla until soft peaks form. Cover and refrigerate until needed.

4. ***Assemble the pie.*** Divide the filling between the crusts, spreading it into an even layer. Arrange the banana slices on top. Spread the whipped cream over the top. Serve immediately or chill until ready to serve.

## Equipment Hack

Use two widemouthed 8-ounce metal canning jar lids or ramekins instead.

## Tip

Add a garnish of sweetened shredded coconut or shaved dark chocolate to the top of the pie.

# Lemon Meringue Mini Pies

EQUIPMENT/TOOLS: PASTRY CUTTER, PLASTIC WRAP, ROLLING PIN,
MINI PIE DISH, PIE WEIGHTS, ELECTRIC MIXER, WIRE RACK

**Makes 2 mini pies • Prep time: 20 minutes, plus 1 hour to chill •
Cook time: 10 minutes • Mini Equipment**

Lemon meringue pie is a sweet, citrusy dream in a piecrust. A thick, tart-sweet lemon custard filling is topped with swirls of sweet meringue toasted to a beautiful golden brown. This sweet little pie is a real showstopper.

**FOR THE CRUST**

½ cup plus 2 tablespoons
    all-purpose flour, plus
    additional for dusting

½ teaspoon sugar

¼ teaspoon kosher salt

¼ cup cold unsalted butter, cut
    into small pieces

1½ to 2 tablespoons ice water

**FOR THE FILLING**

1½ tablespoons cornstarch

⅓ cup sugar

⅛ teaspoon kosher salt

¼ cup water

1 large egg yolk

1 teaspoon freshly grated
    lemon zest

2 tablespoons freshly squeezed
    lemon juice

2 tablespoons unsalted butter

**FOR THE TOPPING**

1 large egg white

Pinch cream of tartar

2 tablespoons sugar

½ teaspoon vanilla extract

1. **Make the crust.** In a medium bowl, whisk together the flour, sugar, and salt. Add the butter. Using a pastry cutter, fork, or two knives, cut the butter into the flour mixture until there are pea-size clumps of dough. Sprinkle 1½ tablespoons of water over the dough and mix until the dough comes together in a ball. If the dough is dry, add additional water, ½ teaspoon at a time, until the dough forms. Flatten the ball into a disk shape and wrap it tightly in plastic wrap. Chill in the refrigerator for 30 minutes.

2. **Preheat the oven and par bake the crust.** Preheat the oven to 375°F. Roll out the chilled dough on a lightly floured surface, about ¼-inch thick. Press the dough into the bottom of the vessel(s) of your choice. Trim off any excess around the edges and crimp the edges. Fill the crust with pie weights or prick the bottom of the crust several times with a fork. Bake for 16 to 18 minutes, until golden brown. Remove from the oven and set aside to cool. Remove the pie weights. Reduce the oven temperature to 325°F.

3. **Make the filling.** In a medium saucepan over medium heat, whisk together the cornstarch, sugar, salt, and water and bring to a boil. Reduce the heat to medium-low and simmer, stirring frequently, until the mixture thickens, about 2 minutes. Remove the pan from the heat. In a small bowl, whisk together the egg yolk with a tablespoon of the sugar mixture. Add another couple of tablespoons of the sugar mixture and stir to combine, then stir the egg yolk mixture into the rest of the sugar mixture in the pan. Set the pan over medium heat and cook, stirring constantly, until the mixture comes to a boil and then continue to cook for 3 minutes more. Remove the pan from the heat and whisk in the lemon zest, lemon juice, and butter until the butter is melted and well incorporated.

4. **Make the topping.** In a medium bowl, use an electric mixer on medium-high to beat the egg white and cream of tartar until the mixture forms soft peaks. Add the sugar and vanilla and continue beating until the mixture forms medium stiff peaks.

5. **Assemble and bake the pie.** Spoon the filling into the piecrust and spread it into an even layer. Spoon the meringue on top and use the back of the spoon to spread it to reach the crust all around and swirl it decoratively. Bake for about 20 minutes, until the meringue topping is golden brown. Let cool completely on a wire rack before serving.

## Equipment Hack

Use two 8-ounce ramekins instead.

## Tip

Stop whipping the meringue when it reaches the medium-stiff-peaks stage, when it stands upright when you lift the whisk out, but the peak still curls over. This will ensure smooth slicing when you go to serve the pie.

# Pumpkin Mini Pies

**EQUIPMENT/TOOLS: FOOD PROCESSOR, MINI PIE DISH, WIRE RACK**

**Makes 2 mini pies • Prep time: 10 minutes, plus 30 minutes to
chill the dough and 1 hour to cool the pie • Cook time: 30 minutes • Mini Equipment**

Pumpkin pie is a must on Thanksgiving, but why reserve this autumnal treat only for large holiday gatherings? This recipe makes a perfect two-person mini pie—a spicy gingersnap-crumb crust filled with a rich pumpkin custard. And because it uses canned pumpkin purée, you can make it any time of year.

**FOR THE CRUST**

12 gingersnaps

2 tablespoons unsalted
   butter, melted

**FOR THE FILLING**

¼ cup plus 1 tablespoon
   canned pumpkin purée

2 tablespoons sugar

1 tablespoon milk

1 large egg

1 teaspoon pumpkin pie spice

Pinch kosher salt

1. ***Preheat the oven and make the crust.*** Preheat the oven to 400°F. In a food processor, pulse the gingersnaps until they are coarse crumbs. Add the butter and pulse to combine. Press the mixture into the bottom and up the sides of two vessels of your choice. Bake for about 10 minutes, until just beginning to brown.

2. ***Make the filling.*** In a medium bowl, whisk together the pumpkin, sugar, milk, egg, pumpkin pie spice, and salt until smooth.

3. ***Assemble and bake the pie.*** Spoon the filling into the par-baked crusts and spread it into an even layer. Bake for 10 minutes, then reduce the heat to 325°F and continue to bake until the filling is set, about 10 minutes more. Let the pie cool on a wire rack before serving.

## Equipment Hack

Use two 8-ounce ramekins instead.

## Tip

You can make your own pumpkin purée out of roasted pumpkin or butternut squash.

# Bourbon Pecan Pie

EQUIPMENT/TOOLS: PASTRY CUTTER, PLASTIC WRAP, ROLLING PIN,
MINI PIE DISH, PIE WEIGHTS, WIRE RACK

**Makes 2 slices • Prep time: 10 minutes, plus 30 minutes to chill the dough •
Cook time: 60 minutes • Mini Equipment**

Dark, sweet caramel, toasted pecans, and a splash of bourbon in this pie make me swoon. It's a classic—a tried-and-true recipe that is perfectly at home on a holiday table. But you don't have to wait for a special occasion to whip up this pie—it's easy to make and delicious any day of the year.

**FOR THE CRUST**

½ cup plus 2 tablespoons
    all-purpose flour, plus
    additional for dusting

½ teaspoon
    granulated sugar

¼ teaspoon kosher salt

¼ cup cold unsalted butter,
    cut into small pieces

1½ to 2 tablespoons ice water

**FOR THE FILLING**

1 large egg

⅓ cup dark brown sugar

¼ cup corn syrup

1½ tablespoons unsalted
    butter, melted

⅛ teaspoon kosher salt

1 tablespoon bourbon

1 cup toasted pecan
    halves, divided

1. ***Make the crust.*** In a medium bowl, whisk together the flour, sugar, and salt. Add the butter and, using a pastry cutter, fork, or two knives, cut in the butter until there are pea-size clumps of dough. Sprinkle 1½ tablespoons of water over the dough and mix until the dough comes together in a ball. If the dough is still dry, add additional water, ½ teaspoon at a time, until it comes together. Flatten the ball into a disk shape and wrap it tightly in plastic wrap. Chill in the refrigerator for 30 minutes.

2. ***Preheat the oven and par-bake the crust.*** Preheat the oven to 350°F. Place the chilled dough on a lightly floured surface and roll it out to a thickness of about ¼ inch. Transfer the dough to your preferred cooking vessel(s), gently press the dough into the bottom, trim off any excess, and crimp the edges. Fill the crust with pie weights or prick the bottom of the crust several times with a fork. Bake for 16 to 18 minutes, until golden brown. Let cool. Remove the pie weights.

3. ***Make the filling.*** In a medium bowl, combine the egg and brown sugar and beat to mix. Add the corn syrup, butter, salt, and bourbon and beat to incorporate. Roughly chop half of the pecans and stir them into the filling mixture.

4. ***Assemble and bake the pie.*** Spoon the filling into the par-baked crust. Place the remaining pecan halves on top in a decorative fashion. Bake for 40 to 45 minutes, until the filling is set. Let cool on a wire rack for at least an hour before serving.

## Equipment Hack

Use two 8-ounce ramekins instead.

## Tip

To toast the pecans, spread them in a single layer on a baking sheet and bake in a pre-heated 350°F oven for 3 to 5 minutes, just until lightly toasted.

# Chocolate Mousse Pie

**EQUIPMENT/TOOLS: FOOD PROCESSOR, MINI PIE DISH,
ELECTRIC MIXER, PLASTIC WRAP**

**Makes 2 slices • Prep time: 10 minutes plus 4 hours to chill •
No-Bake, Mini Equipment**

An easy chocolate cookie-crumb crust is filled with luscious, creamy chocolate mousse topped with lightly sweetened whipped cream. It is a chocolate lover's dream. You can't go wrong serving this to cap off a romantic dinner for two. Think Valentine's Day, date night, or making any regular day into a special occasion.

**FOR THE CRUST**

22 chocolate wafer cookies

2 tablespoons unsalted
   butter, melted

**FOR THE FILLING**

3 ounces semisweet chocolate,
   finely chopped

1½ tablespoons water

2 teaspoons unsweetened
   cocoa powder

1 teaspoon granulated sugar

Pinch kosher salt

½ cup heavy (whipping) cream

1 teaspoon vanilla extract

**FOR THE TOPPING**

½ cup heavy (whipping) cream

1 teaspoon
   confectioners' sugar

Shaved semisweet chocolate
   or cocoa powder, for
   garnish (optional)

1. *Make the crust.* In a food processor, pulse the cookies into fine crumbs. Add the butter and pulse just to incorporate. Press the mixture into the bottom and up the sides of your vessel(s) of choice. Chill in the refrigerator while you make the filling.

2. *Make the filling.* In a medium microwave-safe bowl, combine the chocolate, water, cocoa powder, sugar, and salt. Heat in the microwave in 30-second increments, stirring in between, until the chocolate is completely melted and the mixture is smooth. In another medium bowl, use an electric mixer on medium-high to whip the cream and the vanilla until it holds stiff peaks. Using a rubber spatula, add the whipped cream to the melted chocolate and gently fold the two together.

➤

3. ***Assemble the pie.*** Spoon the filling into the crust and smooth it into an even layer. Cover with plastic wrap and refrigerate for at least 4 hours.

4. ***Make the topping.*** In a medium bowl, use the electric mixer on medium-high to whip the cream and confectioners' sugar into stiff peaks. Swirl the whipped cream on top of the pie before serving. Garnish with shaved chocolate or cocoa powder (if using). Serve.

## Equipment Hack

Use two widemouthed 8-ounce canning jars or ramekins instead.

## Tip

Make it a mocha pie by adding a tablespoon of instant espresso powder to the whipped cream topping.

# Peach Hand Pies

**Makes 2 hand pies • Prep time: 20 minutes, plus 30 minutes to chill the dough • Cook time: 15 to 18 minutes**

When you are craving pie, but want something quicker, hand pies are the perfect solution. These peach-filled pastries are fantastic made with fresh summer peaches, but frozen peaches are great, too, making this an ideal recipe for your year-round baking arsenal.

## FOR THE CRUST
1¼ cups all-purpose flour, plus additional for dusting

1 teaspoon granulated sugar

½ teaspoon kosher salt

½ cup (1 stick) cold unsalted butter, cut into small pieces

3 to 4 tablespoons ice water

## FOR THE FILLING
1 tablespoon unsalted butter

1 tablespoon all-purpose flour

2 peaches, peeled and sliced

¼ cup light brown sugar

½ teaspoon vanilla extract

Pinch kosher salt

1 large egg white beaten with 1 teaspoon of water

1. ***Make the crust.*** In a medium bowl, whisk together the flour, sugar, and salt. Add the butter and, using a pastry cutter, fork, or two knives, cut in the butter until there are pea-size clumps of dough. Sprinkle 3 tablespoons of water over the dough and mix until the dough comes together in a ball. If the dough is still dry, add additional water, 1 teaspoon at a time, until the dough comes together. Flatten the ball into a disk shape and wrap it tightly in plastic wrap. Chill in the refrigerator for 30 minutes.

2. ***Preheat the oven and prepare the pan.*** Preheat the oven to 350°F. Line the baking sheet with parchment paper.

3. ***Make the filling.*** In a medium skillet over medium heat, melt the butter. Stir in the flour, then add the peaches and toss to coat them with the butter. Add the brown sugar, vanilla, and salt and toss to mix. Cook, stirring frequently, until the peaches soften and the liquid is reduced, 3 to 5 minutes. Drain the peaches in a colander or fine-mesh sieve.

**4. Assemble the pies.** Place the chilled dough on a lightly floured surface and roll it out to a thickness of about ¼ inch. Using a large, round cutter or using a small plate or bowl as a guide, cut out two rounds of dough, each 6 to 7 inches in diameter. Divide the filling between each pastry circle. Fold the circles over to encase the filling, crimping the edges together to seal them. Poke or cut a few holes in the top of each pie to allow steam to escape while they bake. Place the pies on the prepared baking sheet and brush them with the egg wash. Bake for 15 to 18 minutes, until golden brown. Let cool on a wire rack for at least 30 minutes before serving.

## Tip

Add a brown sugar glaze to the top of these hand pies to make them extra special. Stir together 1 teaspoon of melted unsalted butter, 2 teaspoons of brown sugar, 2½ tablespoons of confectioners' sugar, and 1 to 2 teaspoons of milk until smooth. Drizzle over the cooled pies and let set for several minutes until the glaze hardens.

# *Strawberry and Dark Chocolate Hand Pies*

EQUIPMENT/TOOLS: PASTRY CUTTER, PLASTIC WRAP, BAKING SHEET,
PARCHMENT PAPER, ROLLING PIN, WIRE RACK

**Makes 2 hand pies • Prep time: 20 minutes, plus 30 minutes to chill the dough •
Cook time: 15 to 18 minutes**

Chocolate-dipped strawberries are a treat that seems perfectly suited to a romantic evening. Putting strawberries and chocolate inside a buttery, flaky piecrust in charming little handheld packages makes them extra special. For Valentine's Day, I like to use a small heart-shaped cookie cutter to cut holes in the top of the hand pies (cut them before you fill and fold the pies).

### FOR THE CRUST
1¼ cups all-purpose flour, plus
  additional for dusting
1 teaspoon granulated sugar
½ teaspoon kosher salt
½ cup (1 stick) cold unsalted
  butter, cut into small pieces
3 to 4 tablespoons ice water

### FOR THE FILLING
1 cup chopped strawberries
1 teaspoon freshly squeezed
  lemon juice
¼ cup sugar
1½ tablespoons cornstarch
1½ ounces chocolate,
  finely chopped

1 large egg beaten with
  1 teaspoon of water
Coarse sugar for
  sprinkling (optional)

1. ***Make the crust.*** In a medium bowl, whisk together the flour, sugar, and salt. Add the butter and, using a pastry cutter, fork, or two knives, cut in the butter until there are pea-size clumps of dough. Sprinkle 3 tablespoons water over the dough and mix until the dough comes together in a ball. If the dough is still dry, add additional water, 1 teaspoon at a time, until the dough comes together. Flatten the ball into a disk shape and wrap it tightly in plastic wrap. Chill in the refrigerator for 30 minutes.

2. ***Preheat the oven and prepare the pan.*** Preheat the oven to 350°F. Line the baking sheet with parchment paper.

➤

3. ***Make the filling.*** In a small bowl, stir together the strawberries and lemon juice and let stand for 10 minutes. Add the sugar and cornstarch and stir to mix well.

4. ***Assemble the pies.*** Place the chilled dough on a lightly floured surface and roll it out to a thickness of about ¼ inch. Using a large, round cutter or using a small plate or bowl as a guide, cut out 2 rounds of dough, 6 to 7 inches in diameter. Divide the filling between each pastry circle. Sprinkle the chopped chocolate over the strawberry filling of each pie. Fold the circles over to encase the filling, crimping the edges together to seal them. Poke or cut a few holes in the top of each pie to allow steam to escape while they bake.

5. ***Bake the pies.*** Place the pies on the prepared baking sheet and brush them with the egg wash and sprinkle a bit of coarse sugar (if using) over the top. Bake for 15 to 18 minutes, until golden brown. Let cool on a wire rack for at least 30 minutes before serving.

## Tip

You can substitute another chocolate-friendly fruit for the strawberries, such as raspberries or bananas.

# No-Bake Key Lime Pie Cups

EQUIPMENT/TOOLS: FOOD PROCESSOR, TWO WIDEMOUTHED
8-OUNCE CANNING JAR LIDS, PLASTIC WRAP

**Makes 2 pie cups • Prep time: 10 minutes, plus 4 hours to chill • No-Bake**

Teeny, tiny key limes have a distinctive floral flavor that really shines in these pie cups. These cute little limes can be hard to come by (and even harder to zest and juice due to their diminutive size). If you can't find them or don't want to bother with juicing them, use freshly squeezed regular (Persian) lime juice and zest instead. The flavor is a bit different, but still delicious.

**FOR THE CRUST**

4 graham cracker sheets

1 tablespoon sugar

1 tablespoon unsalted butter, melted

**FOR THE FILLING**

2½ ounces cream cheese, at room temperature

2 tablespoons freshly squeezed key lime juice

1 teaspoon fresh key lime zest, plus additional for garnish

¼ cup sweetened condensed milk

1. **Make the crust.** In a food processor, pulse the graham crackers with the sugar until they are coarse crumbs. Add the butter and pulse to incorporate. The mixture should be the texture of wet sand. Press the crumb mixture into the bottom of your preferred vessel(s) in an even layer, about ¼- to ½-inch thick. Place in the freezer to chill while you make the filling.

2. **Make the filling.** In a medium bowl, combine the cream cheese, lime juice, lime zest, and condensed milk and beat to combine.

3. **Assemble and chill the cups.** Spoon the filling into the prepared crusts, garnish with lime zest, if desired, cover loosely with plastic wrap, and refrigerate for at least 4 hours. Serve chilled.

## Equipment Hack

Use two 8-ounce ramekins instead.

## Tip

The crust for these can be easily changed up to bring in different flavors. Try using gingersnaps or Nilla Wafers in place of the graham crackers. If the cookies are particularly sweet, you may want to reduce the amount of sugar in the crust.

# Cinnamon Pear Galettes

**EQUIPMENT/TOOLS: PASTRY CUTTER, PLASTIC WRAP, ROLLING PIN, BAKING SHEET, PARCHMENT PAPER, WIRE RACK**

**Makes 2 galettes • Prep time: 15 minutes, plus 30 minutes to chill the dough • Cook time: 15 to 20 minutes**

Like a pie, a galette has a short pastry crust and is often filled with fruit before baking. But a galette is more free-form than a pie. Fruit is piled in the middle of a round of pastry and the pastry is then folded over the edge of the fruit. This version is spiced with cinnamon and filled with juicy pears. It's perfect on its own or topped with a scoop of vanilla ice cream.

**FOR THE CRUST**

1¼ cups all-purpose flour, plus additional for dusting

1 teaspoon granulated sugar

½ teaspoon kosher salt

½ cup (1 stick) cold unsalted butter, cut into small pieces

3 to 4 tablespoons ice water

1 large egg beaten with 1 teaspoon water

**FOR THE FILLING**

2 pears, peeled and sliced

1 tablespoon freshly squeezed lemon juice

3 tablespoons granulated sugar

1 teaspoon cinnamon

2 tablespoons honey

1. ***Make the crust.*** In a medium bowl, whisk together the flour, sugar, and salt. Add the butter and, using a pastry cutter, fork, or two knives, cut in the butter until there are pea-size clumps of dough. Sprinkle 3 tablespoons of water over the dough and mix until the dough comes together in a ball. If the dough is still dry, add additional water, 1 teaspoon at a time, until the dough comes together. Divide the dough into two equal pieces and roll them into balls. Flatten the balls into disks and wrap them tightly in plastic wrap. Chill in the refrigerator for 30 minutes.

2. ***Preheat the oven and make the filling.*** Preheat the oven to 400°F. Line the baking sheet with parchment paper. In a medium bowl, combine the pears, lemon juice, sugar, and cinnamon and toss to coat.

3. ***Assemble the galettes.*** Place the chilled dough on a lightly floured surface and roll out each into rounds about ¼-inch thick. Spread the honey over the rounds. Arrange the sliced pears in the center of each dough round, leaving about 1½ inches of border clear. Fold the edges of the dough up so that they partially cover the pears, leaving the center open and the fruit exposed. Brush the egg wash over the crust. Place on the prepared baking sheet and bake for 15 to 20 minutes, until the pears are soft and the crust is golden brown. Let cool on a wire rack. Serve warm or at room temperature.

# Fig, Honey, and Blue Cheese Galettes

**EQUIPMENT/TOOLS: PASTRY CUTTER, PLASTIC WRAP, BAKING SHEET, PARCHMENT PAPER, ROLLING PIN, WIRE RACK**

**Makes 2 galettes • Prep time: 10 minutes, plus 30 minutes to chill the dough • Cook time: 20 minutes • Lightly Sweet**

These sweet-and-savory galettes combine the cheese course and dessert in one. Sweet, ripe figs and honey are balanced by the pungent, salty bite of Gorgonzola cheese, all nestled in a flaky puff pastry base. These are perfect when you want something just a little sweet.

**FOR THE CRUST**

1 cup all-purpose flour, plus
   additional for dusting

¼ teaspoon kosher salt

¼ teaspoon baking powder

½ cup (1 stick) cold unsalted
   butter, sliced

¼ cup sour cream

1 large egg beaten with
   1 teaspoon of water

**FOR THE FILLING**

2 tablespoons fig jam

4 or 5 medium figs, stemmed
   and sliced about ¼-inch thick

2 tablespoons crumbled
   Gorgonzola cheese

1 tablespoon melted
   butter mixed with
   1 tablespoon honey

1. ***Make the dough.*** In a medium bowl, whisk together the flour, salt, and baking powder. Add the butter and, using a pastry cutter, fork, or two knives, cut the butter into the flour mixture until it is in pea-size pieces. Stir in the sour cream. On a lightly floured surface, knead the dough two or three times until it comes together in a ball. Pat or roll out the dough into a rectangle about ¼-inch thick. Fold the bottom of the dough over about two-thirds of the dough, then fold the other third over the top. Turn the dough 90 degrees and roll it out again into a rectangle. Fold it one more time as before. Wrap it tightly in plastic wrap and chill for at least 30 minutes.

2. ***Preheat the oven and prepare the pan.*** Preheat the oven to 400°F. Line the baking sheet with parchment paper.

3. ***Assemble the galettes.*** Place the chilled dough on a lightly floured surface and cut it in half with a serrated knife. Roll out each into a round that is about 6 inches across. Spread the jam in a thin layer over each round, leaving a clear border of an inch or so. Arrange the fig slices over the jam. Sprinkle the cheese over the figs and then drizzle the honey-and-butter mixture over the top. Fold the edges of the dough up so that it partially covers the figs, leaving the center open and the fruit exposed. Place the galettes on the prepared baking sheet. Brush the egg wash over the crust.

4. ***Bake the galettes.*** Bake for about 30 minutes, until the crust is golden brown. Transfer to a wire rack to cool before serving.

## *Tip*

You can substitute another fruit—pears or apples are good choices—for the figs. If you don't have fig jam, use any type of jam you like. For a bit of crunch, sprinkle a couple tablespoons of chopped walnuts or pecans over the fruit before baking.

# *Lemon Curd Tarts*

**Makes 2 tarts • Prep time: 10 minutes, plus 4 hours to chill •
No-Bake, Mini Equipment**

Tart-sweet lemon curd makes a flavorful filling for a crunchy gingersnap-crumb crust. These no-bake tarts can be made and served in anything from widemouthed canning jar lids to ramekins or even teacups. Since these are a no-bake dessert, you can really be creative about the vessels you use. Just make sure they have edges to hold the filling in.

½ cup gingersnap crumbs

1 tablespoon unsalted
 butter, melted

¼ cup sour cream

¼ cup lemon curd

Sweetened whipped
 cream (optional)

1. ***Make the crust.*** In a small bowl, stir together the gingersnap crumbs and butter. Press the mixture firmly into the bottoms and up the sides of your vessels.

2. ***Make the filling.*** In a small bowl, whisk the sour cream until it is fluffy. Gently fold in the lemon curd.

3. ***Assemble and chill the tarts.*** Spoon the mixture into the crusts. Cover with plastic wrap and chill in the refrigerator for at least 4 hours before serving. Serve chilled, topped with sweetened whipped cream (if desired).

## *Equipment Hack*

Use two widemouthed 8-ounce canning jar lids or ramekins instead.

## *Tip*

You can substitute graham cracker or vanilla wafer crumbs for the gingersnap crumbs if you prefer them.

# Raspberry Jam-Filled Mini Tartlets

EQUIPMENT/TOOLS: PASTRY CUTTER, PLASTIC WRAP, MUFFIN TIN, WIRE RACK

**Makes 2 mini tartlets • Prep time: 15 minutes, plus 30 minutes to chill the dough • Cook time: 16 to 18 minutes • Mini Equipment**

These tiny, jam-filled tartlets could not be any cuter. You can fill them with whatever type of jam you like—strawberry, blackberry, apricot, peach, etc. Raspberries are my favorite and I love the vibrant red color, which makes them a great choice for a special Valentine. Or mix blueberries with raspberries for a festive Fourth of July treat.

½ cup plus 2 tablespoons all-purpose flour

½ teaspoon sugar

¼ teaspoon kosher salt

¼ cup cold unsalted butter, cut into small pieces

1½ to 2 tablespoons ice water

¼ cup raspberry jam

1. **Make the crust.** In a medium bowl, whisk together the flour, sugar, and salt. Add the butter and, using a pastry cutter, fork, or two knives, cut in the butter until there are pea-size clumps of dough. Sprinkle 1½ tablespoons of water over the dough and mix until the dough comes together in a ball. If the dough is still dry, add additional water, ½ teaspoon at a time, until the dough comes together. Flatten the ball into a disk shape and wrap it tightly in plastic wrap. Chill in the refrigerator for 30 minutes.

2. **Preheat the oven and assemble the tartlets.** Preheat the oven to 375°F. Cut the dough into two equal pieces and roll each into a ball. Place on a lightly floured surface and roll out each ball into a circle 4 to 4½ inches across. Press the dough circles into the two wells of your muffin tin. Trim any excess and crimp the edges. Spread 1 tablespoon of jam into each tartlet.

3. **Bake the tartlets.** Bake for 16 to 18 minutes, until the crusts are golden brown. Let cool on a wire rack before unmolding and serving.

## Equipment Hack

Place the dough circles into 4 wells of a mini muffin tin and use the bottom of a shot glass to shape the mini crusts around, or use two widemouthed metal canning jar lids instead.

## Tip

If you have extra pastry dough, you can form the scraps together into a ball. Roll out to ¼-inch thickness and then cut into shapes using miniature cookie cutters, like hearts or stars. Bake these alongside the tarts and then place them on top for decoration.

# Mixed Berry and Pastry Cream Tartlet

EQUIPMENT/TOOLS: PASTRY CUTTER, PLASTIC WRAP, ROLLING PIN, MINI PIE DISH, PIE WEIGHTS, SAUCEPAN, FINE-MESH SIEVE, WIRE RACK

**Makes 2 pieces • Prep time: 15 minutes, plus 30 minutes to chill the dough and 45 to 60 minutes to chill the pastry cream • Cook time: 25 minutes • Mini Equipment**

Learning to make a flaky piecrust and a silky, rich pastry cream will give you culinary superpowers. With these two techniques in your repertoire, you can make all sorts of classic and fanciful desserts. This tartlet is a perfect example. A buttery crust is filled with a luscious, creamy filling, which is topped with gorgeous fresh berries. A light glaze seals in the juices and gives the fruit irresistible shine.

**FOR THE CRUST**

1 cup all-purpose flour, plus additional for dusting

¼ teaspoon kosher salt

¼ teaspoon baking powder

½ cup (1 stick) cold unsalted butter, sliced

¼ cup sour cream

1 large egg beaten with 1 teaspoon of water

**FOR THE PASTRY CREAM**

½ cup whole milk

2 tablespoons plus 1½ teaspoons granulated sugar, divided

1 large egg yolk

1½ teaspoons cornstarch

1½ teaspoons all-purpose flour

1½ teaspoons unsalted butter

½ teaspoon vanilla extract

**FOR THE TOPPING**

1½ cups fresh raspberries

2 tablespoons seedless raspberry jam, red currant jelly, or apricot jam

1. **Make the pastry dough.** In a medium bowl, whisk together the flour, salt, and baking powder. Add the butter and, using a pastry cutter, fork, or two knives, cut the butter into the flour mixture until it is in pea-size pieces. Stir in the sour cream. On a lightly floured surface, knead the dough two or three times until it comes together in a ball. Pat or roll it out into a rectangle about ¼-inch thick. Fold the bottom of the dough over about two-thirds of the dough, then fold the other third over the top. Turn the dough 90 degrees and roll it out again into a rectangle. Fold one more time as before. Wrap it tightly in plastic wrap and chill for at least 30 minutes.

2. **Preheat the oven and prepare the pan.** Preheat the oven to 400°F.

3. ***Par-bake the tart crust.*** Place the chilled dough on a lightly floured surface and roll it out to a round ¼-inch thick. Transfer the dough to your cooking vessel and press it into the sides and bottom. Trim any excess dough. Prick the dough several times with a fork or fill it with pie weights. Bake for about 20 minutes, until the crust is golden brown. Let cool completely in the pan on a wire rack. Remove the pie weights.

4. ***Make the pastry cream.*** In a small saucepan over medium-high heat, combine the milk and 2 tablespoons of the sugar. Bring almost to a boil, then turn off the heat. In a medium bowl, whisk the egg yolk with the remaining 1½ teaspoons of sugar. Whisk in the cornstarch and flour and combine well. While whisking constantly, slowly add the hot milk. Strain through a fine-meshed sieve into a bowl, then return the strained mixture to the saucepan. Cook over medium-high heat, stirring constantly, until it thickens, 1 to 2 minutes. Transfer the mixture to the bowl and stir in the butter and vanilla. Cover with plastic wrap and press it down onto the surface of the cream. Refrigerate for 45 to 60 minutes, until it is completely chilled.

5. ***Assemble the tart.*** Spoon the chilled pastry cream into the cooled tart crust and smooth it into an even layer. Arrange the fruit on top and brush it with the egg wash. Place the jam in a small microwave-safe bowl and microwave for about 20 seconds to thin it. Brush this over the fruit. Serve.

## *Equipment Hack*

Use two widemouthed metal canning jar lids instead.

# Dark Chocolate Cherry Tartlet

**Makes 2 pieces • Prep time: 10 minutes • Cook time: 12 minutes • Quick, Mini Equipment**

Chocolate-covered cherries can set a romantic tone, but this mini dessert takes the combo to new heights. This chocolate cookie-crumb crust filled with dark chocolate ganache and juicy cherries is sure to win over the object of your affection.

**FOR THE CRUST**

22 chocolate
   wafer cookies
2 tablespoons unsalted
   butter, melted

**FOR THE FILLING**

2½ ounces dark chocolate,
   finely chopped
1½ tablespoons unsalted butter
1 tablespoon heavy
   (whipping) cream

1 large egg yolk
½ teaspoon granulated sugar
½ cup fresh or frozen
   pitted cherries

1. ***Preheat the oven and make the crust.*** Preheat the oven to 350°F. In a food processor, pulse the cookies into fine crumbs. Add the butter and pulse just to incorporate. Press the mixture into the bottom and up the sides of your vessel(s).

2. ***Make the filling.*** In a medium microwave-safe bowl, combine the chocolate and butter. Microwave in 30-second intervals, stirring in between each, until the chocolate is completely melted and the mixture is smooth. Stir in the cream. In a small bowl, whisk together the egg yolk and sugar. Add this to the chocolate mixture and stir to combine well.

3. ***Fill and bake the tart.*** Pour the chocolate mixture into the prepared crust. Bake for 6 minutes. Remove from the oven and reduce the oven temperature to 300°F. Scatter the cherries over the top of the filling. Return the tart to the oven and bake for another 6 minutes. Let cool on a wire rack before serving.

## Tip

Instead of the chocolate cookie-crumb crust, you can use a regular short pastry crust. You'll want to par-bake the crust for about 20 minutes, until it is golden brown, before filling.

# Brown Sugar Cinnamon Stuffed Apple Crisp

EQUIPMENT/TOOLS: PASTRY CUTTER, SAUCEPAN, BAKING SHEET

**Makes 2 apples • Prep time: 15 minutes • Cook time: 25 minutes • Lightly Sweet**

I get a kick out of any food that includes an edible serving vessel. Stuffed, baked apples with a sweet, crumbly topping make a beautiful dessert that's festive enough for a special occasion, but simple enough to have any time. Serve the apples warm topped with a scoop of vanilla or caramel ice cream. For extra crunch, add 2 tablespoons of chopped walnuts or pecans to the topping mixture.

## FOR THE TOPPING

¼ cup all-purpose flour

2 tablespoons old-fashioned rolled oats

2 tablespoons light brown sugar

⅛ teaspoon kosher salt

½ teaspoon cinnamon

2 tablespoons cold unsalted butter, cut into small pieces

## FOR THE APPLES

4 apples, divided

2 tablespoons unsalted butter

2 tablespoons light brown sugar

½ teaspoon cinnamon

1. ***Preheat the oven and make the topping.*** Preheat oven to 400°F. In a medium bowl, combine the flour, oats, brown sugar, salt, and cinnamon and mix well. Add the butter and use a pastry cutter, fork, or two knives to cut the butter into the oat mixture.

2. ***Make the filling.*** Peel, core, and dice 2 of the apples. In a small saucepan over medium heat, combine the chopped apples, butter, brown sugar, and cinnamon and cook until the apples are tender, about 10 minutes.

3. ***Prepare and stuff the apples.*** Slice the tops off the 2 remaining apples and use a melon baller or a small spoon to hollow them out, making enough room inside for the filling. Spoon the filling mixture into the apples. Place the stuffed apples on a baking sheet and top them with the topping mixture.

4. ***Bake the apples.*** Bake for 12 to 14 minutes, until the filling and apples are hot and the topping is crisp. Serve warm.

# Pear and Coconut Crisp

**Makes 2 crisps** · **Prep time: 5 minutes** · **Cook time: 20 to 25 minutes** ·
**Quick, Lightly Sweet**

Pears bake down to a bubbling, sweet compote, which makes them a great fruit for a crisp. The toasted topping is sweet, crunchy, and just a little bit chewy from the coconut—a perfect combination.

Unsalted butter, at room
   temperature, for preparing
   the ramekins

**FOR THE FILLING**

2 pears, cored and sliced

2 tablespoons
   granulated sugar

1 teaspoon freshly squeezed
   lemon juice

**FOR THE TOPPING**

½ cup old-fashioned
   rolled oats

2½ tablespoons light
   brown sugar

2 tablespoons unsweetened
   shredded coconut

1 tablespoon all-purpose flour

¼ teaspoon cinnamon

2 tablespoons cold unsalted
   butter, cut into small pieces

1. **Preheat the oven and prepare the ramekins.** Preheat the oven to 400°F. Grease the vessels with butter.

2. **Prepare the filling.** In a medium bowl, toss the pears with the granulated sugar and lemon juice. Place the pears in the prepared vessels.

3. **Prepare the topping.** In a small bowl, stir together the oats, brown sugar, coconut, flour, and cinnamon. Add the butter and, using a pastry cutter, fork, or two knives, cut the butter into the oat mixture. Spoon the topping mixture over the filling.

4. **Bake the crisps.** Bake for 20 to 25 minutes, until the filling is hot and bubbling and the topping is golden brown and crisp. Serve warm.

# Blackberry Cobbler

**Makes 2 servings • Prep time: 10 minutes • Cook time: 1 hour • Mini Equipment**

While crumbles and crisps generally consist of fresh fruits baked with a streusel-like topping, a cobbler is more of a cake or biscuit batter baked with fresh fruit. This mini version pairs a sweet cake batter with juicy blackberries. Serve it topped with either whipped cream or vanilla ice cream.

Unsalted butter, at room temperature, for preparing the loaf pan

½ cup plus 2 tablespoons granulated sugar, divided

½ cup all-purpose flour

½ cup whole milk

2 tablespoons unsalted butter, melted

¾ teaspoon baking powder

⅛ teaspoon salt

1 cup fresh or frozen blackberries

1. ***Preheat the oven and prepare the pan.*** Preheat the oven to 350°F. Grease your cooking vessel(s) with unsalted butter at room temperature.

2. ***Make the batter.*** In a medium bowl, whisk ½ cup of sugar with the flour and milk. Add the butter, baking powder, and salt and whisk to combine.

3. ***Assemble the cobbler.*** Pour the batter into the prepared vessel(s), then scatter the berries over the top. Sprinkle the remaining 2 tablespoons sugar over the top. Bake for about 1 hour, until the cobbler is bubbling and the top is golden brown. Serve warm.

## Equipment Hack

Use two 8-ounce ramekins instead.

## Tip

You can add a streusel topping to this cobbler if you like. Stir together ¼ cup of light brown sugar and ¼ cup of all-purpose flour. Cut in 2 tablespoons of diced, cold unsalted butter. Sprinkle this mixture over the top of the cobbler before baking.

# *Bourbon Peach Cobbler*

**Makes 2 servings** • **Prep time: 10 minutes** • **Cook time: 1 hour** • **Mini Equipment**

The combination of bourbon and peaches always makes me think of sultry, hot summer nights. This simple cobbler is loaded with flavorful fresh peaches and spiked with a hearty shot of bourbon, so it's perfect for setting the tone.

Unsalted butter, at room
temperature, for preparing
the loaf pan

**FOR THE FRUIT FILLING**

3 peaches, peeled and diced

1½ tablespoons bourbon

¼ cup granulated sugar, plus
additional for sprinkling
on top

1 teaspoon cornstarch

½ teaspoon cinnamon

**FOR THE BATTER**

½ cup plus 2 tablespoons
granulated sugar, divided

½ cup all-purpose flour

½ cup whole milk

2 tablespoons unsalted
butter, melted

¾ teaspoon baking powder

⅛ teaspoon salt

1. **Preheat the oven and prepare the pan.** Preheat the oven to 375°F. Grease your cooking vessel(s) with unsalted butter at room temperature.

2. **Prepare the fruit filling.** In the prepared vessel(s), combine the peaches, bourbon, sugar, cornstarch, and cinnamon and toss to coat.

3. **Make the batter.** In a medium bowl, whisk ½ cup of sugar with the flour and milk. Add the butter, baking powder, and salt and whisk to combine.

4. **Assemble and bake the cobbler.** Pour the batter over the fruit filling. Sprinkle the remaining 2 tablespoons of sugar over the top. Bake for about 1 hour, until the cobbler is bubbling and the top is golden brown. Serve warm.

## *Equipment Hack*

Use two 8-ounce ramekins instead.

# Strawberry Rhubarb Crumble

**Makes 2 servings • Prep time: 10 minutes • Cook time: 1 hour • Mini Equipment**

Sweet strawberries and puckery rhubarb bring out the fruity best in each other, and this rustic crumble showcases the combo perfectly. With its lovely pink fruit filling and crunchy topping, this crumble makes an ideal ending to a spring lunch or the first barbecue of the year.

Unsalted butter, at room temperature, for preparing the loaf pan

**FOR THE FRUIT FILLING**

1 cup diced strawberries

¾ cup diced rhubarb

3 tablespoons honey

1 tablespoon cornstarch

½ teaspoon vanilla extract

**FOR THE TOPPING**

⅓ cup all-purpose flour

¼ cup light brown sugar

Pinch kosher salt

2 tablespoons unsalted butter, melted

1. ***Preheat the oven and prepare the pan.*** Preheat the oven to 350°F. Grease the cooking vessel(s) with unsalted butter at room temperature.

2. ***Prepare the fruit filling.*** In the prepared cooking vessel(s), combine the strawberries, rhubarb, honey, cornstarch, and vanilla and toss to mix.

3. ***Prepare the topping.*** In a medium bowl, whisk together the flour, brown sugar, and salt. Add the butter and combine to create a crumbly topping. Pour the topping over the fruit filling and spread into an even layer.

4. ***Bake the crumble.*** Bake for about 1 hour, until the filling bubbles and the topping is golden brown. Serve warm.

## Equipment Hack

Use two 8-ounce ramekins instead.

## Tip

Try different combinations of fruits in this crumble. Blueberry and peach is another great combination.

# 6

# PASTRIES AND CONFECTIONS

Chocolate-Covered Strawberry Cheesecake Bites

**PAGE 131**

When you are craving something a bit different from the usual cookies, cake, or ice cream, fanciful pastries and whimsical confections are a fun way to go. If you're in the mood for a sweet breakfast or brunch treat, try Chocolate-Hazelnut Filled Scones or Maple-Glazed Donuts. Or, if you love little delicacies but hate buying them in bulk, you're in luck—this chapter also offers sweets like Lemon White Chocolate Truffles, Dark Chocolate Almond Butter Cups, and Pecan Brittle. Choose your pick!

Chocolate-Hazelnut Filled Scones **122**

Coffee and Cinnamon Rolls **124**

Maple-Glazed Donuts **126**

Cinnamon Sugar Monkey Bread **127**

Strawberry Shortcakes **129**

Easy Palmiers **130**

Chocolate-Covered Strawberry
   Cheesecake Bites **131**

Lemon White Chocolate Truffles **132**

Classic Chocolate Truffles with Hazelnuts **133**

Dark Chocolate Almond Butter Cups **134**

Stay-at-Home S'mores **135**

White Chocolate and
   Toasted Almond Fudge **137**

Rocky Road Fudge **138**

Peppermint Chocolate Bark **139**

Dark Chocolate Cherry Almond Bark **140**

Pecan Brittle **141**

# Chocolate-Hazelnut Filled Scones

EQUIPMENT/TOOLS: PASTRY CUTTER, ROLLING PIN, PLASTIC WRAP,
BAKING SHEET, PARCHMENT PAPER

**Makes 2 scones • Prep time: 10 minutes, plus 1 hour to chill the dough •
Cook time: 20 to 24 minutes**

Buttery rich scones filled with a chocolate and hazelnut spread are more decadent than the type of scone you'd normally enjoy first thing in the morning, although I would never discourage anyone from enjoying this perfect dessert for breakfast. It is an ideal match for that first hot cup of coffee in the morning or for an after-dinner espresso.

½ cup all-purpose flour, plus additional for dusting

2 tablespoons granulated sugar

½ teaspoon baking powder

⅛ teaspoon kosher salt

2 tablespoons cold unsalted butter, cut into small pieces

¼ cup heavy (whipping) cream

2 tablespoons chocolate-hazelnut spread (like Nutella)

1 large egg yolk beaten with a splash of cream or milk

1 tablespoon coarse sugar, for sprinkling

1. **Make the dough.** In a medium bowl, whisk together the flour, sugar, baking powder, and salt. Cut the butter into the flour using a pastry cutter, fork, or two knives until the mixture is in pea-size clumps. Add the cream and mix with your hands until the mixture comes together in a ball.

2. **Form and fill the scones.** Divide the dough into two pieces. Place on a lightly floured surface and roll out each into an oval until about ¼-inch thick. Spread 1 tablespoon of the chocolate hazelnut spread on each piece of dough. Working from the longer end of the oval, roll the dough into logs, then curl the logs around into spirals. Roll or pat the spirals into disks about 4 inches across. Brush the egg wash over the disks and sprinkle them with the coarse sugar. Wrap tightly in plastic wrap and refrigerate for 1 hour.

3. *Preheat the oven and prepare the pan.* Preheat the oven to 375°F. Line the baking sheet with parchment paper.

4. *Bake the scones.* Bake for 20 to 24 minutes, until the tops are golden brown. Serve warm or let cool to room temperature.

## Tip

You can make the dough in a food processor if you like. Pulse the butter into the dry ingredients until pea-size clumps form, then add the cream and pulse until the mixture comes together in a ball.

# Coffee and Cinnamon Rolls

**Makes 4 rolls • Prep time: 10 minutes, plus 30 minutes to chill the dough • Cook time: 12 to 14 minutes**

I know cinnamon rolls are the kind of thing you normally eat for breakfast, but these are so decadent that even if you're a sweets-in-the-morning person, you'll probably want to save these for dessert. They're classic cinnamon rolls rolled around a sweet cinnamon sugar filling and they're topped with a confectioners' sugar glaze spiked with espresso powder.

**FOR THE DOUGH**

1 cup all-purpose flour, plus
   additional for dusting

¼ teaspoon kosher salt

¼ teaspoon baking powder

½ cup cold unsalted butter,
   cut into small pieces

¼ cup sour cream

1 large egg beaten with
   1 teaspoon of water

**FOR THE FILLING**

2 tablespoons unsalted butter,
   at room temperature

¼ cup light brown sugar

¾ teaspoon cinnamon

**FOR THE GLAZE**

½ cup confectioners' sugar

½ teaspoon instant
   espresso powder

1½ tablespoons milk,
   half-and-half, or heavy
   (whipping) cream

¼ teaspoon vanilla extract

Pinch kosher salt

1. **Make the dough.** In a medium bowl, whisk together the flour, salt, and baking powder. Add the butter and, using a pastry cutter, fork, or two knives, cut the butter into the flour mixture until it is in pea-size pieces. Stir in the sour cream. Place the dough on a lightly floured surface and knead it until it comes together in a ball, about 3 minutes. Pat or roll out the dough into a rectangle about ¼-inch thick. Fold the bottom of the dough over about two-thirds of the dough, then fold the other third over the top. Turn the dough 90 degrees and roll it out again into a rectangle. Fold the dough one more time as before. Wrap it tightly in plastic wrap and chill for at least 30 minutes.

2. **Preheat the oven and prepare the pan.** Preheat the oven to 400°F. Line the baking sheet with parchment paper.

3. **Make the filling.** In a small bowl, whisk together the butter, brown sugar, and cinnamon.

4. **Assemble the rolls.** Place the chilled dough on a lightly floured surface. Roll out the dough into a rectangle about ¼-inch thick. Spread the filling evenly over the top. Starting with one of the short sides of the rectangle, roll the dough into a log. Using a serrated knife, cut the log crosswise into quarters. Place the rolls cut-side down on the prepared baking sheet with space in between. Brush the egg wash over the rolls.

5. **Bake the rolls.** Bake for 12 to 14 minutes, until the pastry is golden brown. Let cool briefly on the baking sheet while you make the glaze.

6. **Make the glaze.** In a small bowl, stir together the confectioners' sugar, espresso powder, milk, vanilla, and salt. Drizzle the glaze generously over the warm rolls. Serve.

## *Tip*

You can substitute 1 sheet (½ package) of store-bought frozen puff pastry for the dough. For the best flavor, look for puff pastry that is made with butter instead of vegetable shortening.

# Maple-Glazed Donuts

EQUIPMENT/TOOLS: NONSTICK COOKING SPRAY, PLASTIC WRAP,
PARCHMENT PAPER, SAUCEPAN

**Makes 2 donuts • Prep time: 10 minutes, plus 2½ hours to rise • Cook time: 12 minutes**

Walking into a donut shop is dangerous. Who can order just one or two? Instead, when I get a craving, I make this small-batch recipe at home. It totally satisfies my donut lust without completely blowing my commitment to moderation. You can top with chocolate ganache (page 58) if preferred.

**FOR THE DONUTS**

1½ tablespoons warm water
¾ teaspoon quick-rise yeast
1 tablespoon sugar
1½ tablespoons buttermilk
Pinch kosher salt

½ cup all-purpose flour, plus
   additional for dusting
¼ teaspoon baking soda
Cooking oil, for frying

**FOR THE GLAZE**

¾ cup confectioners' sugar
2 tablespoons maple syrup

1. ***Make the dough.*** In a medium bowl, stir together the water, yeast, and sugar. Let stand for about 10 minutes, until the mixture becomes foamy. Stir in the buttermilk and salt. Add the flour and baking soda and stir with a fork to mix well. Use your hands to knead the dough into a firm ball (it should be sticky). Wash the bowl and then coat it with a bit of nonstick cooking spray. Place the dough in the bowl, cover with plastic wrap, and set aside in a warm place to rise until it has doubled in size, about 2 hours.

2. ***Form the donuts and let rise again.*** Divide the dough into 4 equal pieces. On a lightly floured surface, roll each piece into a ¼-inch-thick rope. Shape the rope into a ring, pressing the ends together to seal. Place the rings on a sheet of parchment paper, cover with plastic wrap, and set aside for 30 minutes to rise a second time.

3. ***Fry the donuts.*** Line the plate with paper towels. Fill a medium saucepan with about 1 inch of cooking oil. Place over medium-high heat until the oil begins to shimmer. Gently lower the donuts into the oil, cooking one or two at a time depending on the size of your pot, and cook for about 30 seconds per side, until dark golden brown. Transfer to the prepared plate and repeat with the remaining donuts.

4. ***Make and add the glaze.*** In a small bowl, stir together the confectioners' sugar and maple syrup until smooth. Drop the warm donuts in the glaze and turn to coat. Serve warm or at room temperature.

# Cinnamon Sugar Monkey Bread

EQUIPMENT/TOOLS: MINI LOAF PAN, PASTRY CUTTER

**Makes 2 servings • Prep time: 10 minutes • Cook time: 16 to 18 minutes •
Mini Equipment, Quick**

Monkey bread made from scratch has to be one of life's most sinful indulgences. Hot out of the oven, ooey gooey, sugar-and-cinnamon-coated pull-apart pieces of biscuit dough bathed in caramel are impossible to resist. This recipe makes just enough for a decadent dessert for two, and I promise you, no monkeys will be harmed in the process.

Unsalted butter, at room
    temperature, for preparing
    the loaf pan

**FOR THE BISCUITS**

1 cup all-purpose flour

1¼ teaspoons baking powder

¼ teaspoon baking soda

Pinch kosher salt

¼ cup cold unsalted butter, cut
    into small pieces

½ cup buttermilk

**FOR THE TOPPING**

5 tablespoons
    granulated sugar

1½ teaspoons cinnamon

3 tablespoons unsalted
    butter, melted

1. ***Preheat the oven and prepare the pan.*** Preheat the oven to 375°F. Grease your cooking vessel(s) with butter.

2. ***Make the biscuit dough.*** In a medium bowl, whisk together the flour, baking powder, baking soda, and salt. Add the butter and, using a pastry cutter, fork, or your fingers, cut in the butter until it is well incorporated. Stir in the buttermilk and mix just until it comes together in a ball.

3. ***Make the topping.*** In a shallow bowl, stir together the granulated sugar and cinnamon.

➤

4. **Assemble the monkey bread.** Separate the dough into four equal pieces and then divide each of those pieces into three balls. Roll each ball in the cinnamon sugar to coat and place them in the prepared pan. Stir the remaining cinnamon sugar into the butter and pour this over the biscuits.

5. **Bake the monkey bread.** Bake for 16 to 18 minutes, until puffed and golden. Serve warm.

## Equipment Hack

Use 4 wells of a muffin tin instead.

## Tip

For a quicker version, use canned, refrigerated biscuit dough. Half a can will be plenty for this recipe. You could save the other half for breakfast, but I recommend just doubling the recipe because, really, no amount of monkey bread will ever truly be enough.

# Strawberry Shortcakes

**Makes 2 shortcakes • Prep time: 15 minutes • Cook time: 16 to 18 minutes**

Tender biscuits are layered with juicy fresh strawberries and fluffy whipped cream for a dessert that is perfect for a warm spring or summer evening. This is the kind of dessert that absolutely must be assembled just before devouring, so it's ideal for the small-batch treatment.

**FOR THE STRAWBERRIES**

8 ounces strawberries, hulled and quartered

1½ tablespoons granulated sugar

**FOR THE BISCUITS**

⅔ cup all-purpose flour

1¼ teaspoons baking powder

⅛ teaspoon baking soda

1½ teaspoons granulated sugar

¼ teaspoon kosher salt

½ cup heavy (whipping) cream

**FOR THE WHIPPED CREAM**

½ cup cold heavy (whipping) cream

1 tablespoon granulated sugar

½ teaspoon vanilla extract

1. **Prepare the strawberries.** Place the strawberries in a medium bowl and sprinkle the sugar over the top. Toss gently to mix. Set aside.

2. **Preheat the oven and prepare the baking sheet.** Preheat the oven to 400°F. Line the baking sheet with parchment paper.

3. **Make the biscuits.** In another medium bowl, whisk together the flour, baking powder, baking soda, sugar, and salt. Add the cream and stir to combine. Split the dough in two and form the two pieces into rounds about 2 inches thick. Place the rounds on the prepared baking sheet. Bake for 16 to 18 minutes, until golden brown. Let cool on a wire rack while you whip the cream.

4. **Whip the cream.** In a medium bowl, use an electric mixer on medium-high to whip the cream, sugar, and vanilla until soft peaks form.

5. **Assemble the shortcakes.** Split each biscuit horizontally. Divide the strawberries between the bottom halves of each biscuit. Pour any remaining strawberry juice from the bowl over the cut sides of the top halves of the biscuits. Be very gentle when whisking, as overworking the dough can lead to a tougher consistency. Add a large dollop of whipped cream on top of the strawberries, and then top with the other two biscuit halves. Serve immediately.

# *Easy Palmiers*

........................................................................................

**EQUIPMENT/TOOLS: PASTRY CUTTER, PLASTIC WRAP, BAKING SHEET, PARCHMENT PAPER, ROLLING PIN**

........................................................................................

**Makes 2 palmiers • Prep time: 30 minutes, plus 1 hour to chill the dough •
Cook time: 9 to 11 minutes**

These delicate puff pastries are usually formed by rolling up a rectangle of dough from both sides so that the rolls meet in the middle. The resulting log is then sliced into thin slabs that have the shape of palm fronds. When you're making just two of them, the easiest way to get this effect is to twirl ropes of pastry dough into the palm frond shape and roll it flat before baking.

| | | |
|---|---|---|
| ⅓ cup cold unsalted butter, cut into small pieces | ½ cup all-purpose flour, plus additional for dusting | ¼ cup demerara or other coarse sugar, divided |
| | 2½ tablespoons sour cream | |

1. ***Make the dough.*** In a medium bowl, cut the butter into the flour using a pastry cutter, fork, or two knives until the mixture forms pea-size clumps. Stir in the sour cream until the dough comes together in a ball. Wrap the dough tightly in plastic wrap and chill in the refrigerator for at least 1 hour.

2. ***Preheat the oven and prepare the pan.*** Preheat the oven to 450°F. Line the baking sheet with parchment paper.

3. ***Form the palmiers.*** Split the dough into two equal pieces and place on a lightly floured surface. Using your palms, roll out each piece into long ropes, about ½-inch thick. Sprinkle the ropes with the sugar. Lay one of the ropes out flat on the work surface and roll the two ends inward to make spirals that meet in the middle. Using a rolling pin, roll the spirals until about ¼-inch thick. Repeat with the other rope. Place the palmiers on the prepared baking sheet.

4. ***Bake the palmiers.*** Bake for 6 minutes, flip the palmiers over, and bake for another 3 to 5 minutes, until they are crisp and golden brown. Serve warm or at room temperature.

## *Tip*

I like to use demerara sugar for these because of the nice crunch you get from the coarse grains. You can use any coarse-grained sugar—like turbinado or raw sugar—or regular granulated sugar if you like.

# Chocolate-Covered Strawberry Cheesecake Bites

EQUIPMENT/TOOLS: ICE CUBE TRAY

**Makes 6 cheesecake bites** • **Prep time: 10 minutes, plus 20 minutes to chill** • **Quick, No-Bake**

These pretty confections combine many fantastic desserts into one sweet little handheld package. A rich, strawberry-studded cheesecake center is encased in dark chocolate for a dessert that looks like it came from a fancy chocolate shop.

5 ounces semisweet baking chocolate, chopped

4 ounces cream cheese, at room temperature

¼ cup confectioners' sugar

½ teaspoon vanilla extract

2 tablespoons heavy (whipped) cream

3 strawberries, diced

1. **Make the chocolate cups.** In a medium microwave-safe bowl, heat the chocolate in 30-second intervals, stirring in between, until it is completely melted and smooth. Put a scant tablespoonful of the chocolate into each of six wells of your vessel, then tilt and turn so that the chocolate coats the sides. Place in the freezer while you make the filling.

2. **Make the filling.** In a medium bowl, beat the cream cheese, confectioners' sugar, and vanilla until smooth. Add the cream and beat to incorporate. Using a rubber spatula, fold in the strawberries.

3. **Assemble the bites.** Fill each dessert vessel most of the way full with the filling. Spoon more chocolate on top to cover the filling (reheat the chocolate if needed). Freeze until set, about 20 minutes, or refrigerate for 1 hour.

4. **Serve the bites.** To serve, invert the vessels onto a plate and press gently to pop out the cheesecake bites. Let the bites stand at room temperature for about 10 minutes before serving. Store any leftovers in an airtight container in the refrigerator or freezer.

## Equipment Hack

Use chocolate molds or mini foil cupcake liners instead.

# Lemon White Chocolate Truffles

**EQUIPMENT/TOOLS: PARCHMENT PAPER**

**Makes 6 truffles · Prep time: 15 minutes, plus 4 hours and 15 minutes to chill · No-Bake**

Everyone is impressed by a chocolate truffle, but I'm even more impressed by how fun and easy they are to make. These combine the delicate flavor of white chocolate with the tartness of lemon. Coat them in white sparkling sugar, and they look like bejeweled treasures.

3 ounces white chocolate, finely chopped

2 tablespoons heavy (whipping) cream

2 tablespoons unsalted butter, cut into pieces

½ teaspoon grated lemon zest

2 tablespoons white sparkling sugar

1. **Melt the chocolate.** In a small, microwave-safe bowl, combine the chocolate, cream, butter, and lemon zest. Microwave in 30-second intervals, stirring in between, until the chocolate is completely melted and the mixture is smooth. Chill in the refrigerator for at least 4 hours or overnight.

2. **Form the truffles.** Line a plate with parchment paper. Use a small ice cream scoop or a tablespoon to scoop the chocolate mixture and form it into balls. Set the balls on the prepared plate, then chill in the refrigerator for 15 minutes. Place the sparkling sugar on a small plate and roll the balls in it to coat all around. Serve immediately or store in an airtight container for up to a week.

## Tip

Instead of sparkling sugar, you can coat your truffles with finely chopped almonds or hazelnuts, or toasted shredded coconut.

# Classic Chocolate Truffles with Hazelnuts

**Makes 6 truffles • Prep time: 15 minutes, plus 4 hours and 15 minutes to chill • No-Bake**

These are classic truffles made of fine semisweet chocolate and rolled in hazelnuts. They make a perfect little sweet bite without being fussy or difficult to make. The truffles are divine alongside a hot cup of strong coffee or espresso.

3 ounces semisweet chocolate, finely chopped

2 tablespoons heavy (whipping) cream

2 tablespoons unsalted butter, cut into pieces

2 tablespoons finely chopped hazelnuts

1. **Melt the chocolate.** In a small microwave-safe bowl, combine the chocolate, cream, and butter. Microwave in 30-second intervals, stirring in between, until the chocolate is completely melted and the mixture is smooth. Chill in the refrigerator for at least 4 hours or overnight.

2. **Form the truffles.** Line a plate with parchment paper. Use a small ice cream scoop or a tablespoon to scoop the chocolate and form it into balls. Set the balls on the prepared plate, then chill in the refrigerator for 15 minutes. Place the chopped nuts on a small plate and roll the balls in it to coat all around. Serve immediately or store in an airtight container for up to a week.

## Tip

The melted chocolate must be thoroughly chilled before forming the truffles, but don't try to save time by sticking it in the freezer as that will cause it to freeze unevenly.

# *Dark Chocolate Almond Butter Cups*

**EQUIPMENT/TOOLS: MUFFIN TIN, FOIL CUPCAKE LINERS**

**Makes 6 cups · Prep time: 10 minutes, plus 20 minutes to chill · No-Bake · Quick**

Warning: These dark chocolate almond butter cups are dangerously easy to make. The ingredients are things you likely have in your pantry already (if you don't have almond butter, you can substitute another nut butter like peanut). They can also be prepared in less time than it would take you to run out and buy a package of Reese's Peanut Butter Cups. Once you master this recipe, you'll never have to suffer through another evening fighting a candy craving.

3 ounces semisweet chocolate, finely chopped

¼ cup almond butter

2 tablespoons confectioners' sugar

Pinch kosher salt

1. ***Prepare the pan.*** Line 6 wells of a muffin tin with cupcake liners.

2. ***Make the chocolate cups.*** Place the chocolate in a small microwave-safe bowl. Microwave in 30-second intervals, stirring between each, until the chocolate is melted and smooth. Fill the bottom of each cupcake liner with about 1 tablespoon of the melted chocolate. Place in the refrigerator or freezer to set, about 5 minutes.

3. ***Make the filling.*** In a small bowl, stir together the almond butter, sugar, and salt until smooth. Place a scant tablespoon of filling into each cup, using the back of the spoon to gently pat the filling flat.

4. ***Make the chocolate tops.*** If necessary, rewarm the chocolate for a few seconds in the microwave. Spoon this chocolate over the top of the filling, spreading it to completely cover the filling. Place in the refrigerator to set, about 15 minutes. Serve immediately or store in an airtight container in the refrigerator for up to 2 weeks.

## *Tip*

These candies can be made in endless varieties. Try making them with milk chocolate or white chocolate. Or add cinnamon or other flavors to the nut butter. Or substitute a spoonful of caramel sauce for the nut butter.

# Stay-at-Home S'mores

EQUIPMENT/TOOLS: BAKING SHEET, PARCHMENT PAPER, ELECTRIC MIXER, PLASTIC WRAP, ROLLING PIN, COOKIE CUTTER, WIRE RACK

**Makes 2 s'mores • Prep time: 15 minutes, plus 30 minutes to chill • Cook time: 13 minutes**

In my mind, nothing beats a toasty s'more by a campfire. They're messy and sweet and taste like the carefree summer nights of childhood. But let's face it, that one time a year you make it camping is not enough to keep the craving for a chocolate-and-marshmallow graham cracker sandwich at bay. These "stay-at-home" s'mores are a fun way to enjoy the spirit of a campfire s'more in the comfort of your home. Plus, you'll get lots of bonus points for the homemade graham crackers.

**FOR THE GRAHAM CRACKERS**

2 tablespoons unsalted butter

2 tablespoons brown sugar

1 tablespoon corn syrup

¼ teaspoon baking soda

1 cup all-purpose flour, plus additional for dusting

1 tablespoon water

**FOR THE S'MORES**

½ cup mini marshmallows

2 ounces semisweet chocolate

1. ***Preheat the oven and prepare the pan.*** Preheat the oven to 375°F. Line the baking sheet with parchment paper.

2. ***Make the graham crackers.*** In a medium bowl, using an electric mixer on medium-high, cream together the butter, brown sugar, and corn syrup, about 3 minutes. Add the baking soda, flour, and water and mix until the dough comes together in a ball. Wrap tightly in plastic wrap and chill in the refrigerator for at least 30 minutes. Place the chilled dough on a lightly floured surface. Using a rolling pin, roll out the dough to about ⅛-inch thick. Use a cookie cutter to cut out four circular, square, or rectangular crackers. Carefully transfer the crackers to the prepared baking sheet. Bake for about 8 minutes, until the graham crackers are crisp and beginning to brown. Transfer two of the graham crackers to a wire rack, leaving the other two on the baking sheet. Turn on the broiler and move an oven rack to the highest position in the oven.

➤

3. ***Toast the marshmallows.*** Divide the marshmallows between the two graham crackers on the baking sheet. Top each cracker with half of the marshmallows. Place the baking sheet under the broiler and heat until the marshmallows are soft and golden brown, 2 to 3 minutes. Remove from the oven and immediately press the other two graham crackers on top of the marshmallows.

4. ***Dip in chocolate.*** Place a piece of parchment paper on a plate. In a small microwave-safe bowl, microwave the chocolate in 30-second intervals, stirring in between, until the chocolate is completely melted and smooth. One at a time, hold each sandwich between your fingers and dip it halfway into the chocolate. Place it on the prepared plate and repeat with the second sandwich. Chill in the refrigerator until the chocolate sets, about 30 minutes. Serve at room temperature or store in an airtight container on the countertop.

## Tip

Homemade graham crackers are a definite treat, but feel free to use store-bought graham crackers in place of the homemade version. You might even choose to use cinnamon or chocolate graham crackers.

# White Chocolate and Toasted Almond Fudge

EQUIPMENT/TOOLS: MINI MUFFIN TIN, NONSTICK COOKING SPRAY

**Makes 6 pieces of fudge** • **Prep time: 5 minutes, plus 2 hours to chill** •
**Mini Equipment, No-Bake**

This fudge is ridiculously easy to make. The chocolate is melted in the microwave, but other than that there's no cooking involved. The result is a rich, smooth white chocolate fudge studded with toasted almonds.

| | | |
|---|---|---|
| 2 ounces white chocolate, finely chopped | ¼ cup sweetened condensed milk | ¼ cup chopped toasted almonds |
| | ⅛ teaspoon vanilla extract | |

1. ***Prepare the pan.*** Grease your dessert vessels with nonstick cooking spray.

2. ***Make the fudge.*** In a medium microwave-safe bowl, combine the chocolate and sweetened condensed milk. Microwave in 30-second intervals, stirring in between, until the chocolate is completely melted and the mixture is smooth. Stir in the vanilla and nuts. Divide the mixture among the six wells of the tin.

3. ***Chill and serve.*** Refrigerate until set, at least 2 hours. Serve immediately or store in an airtight container at room temperature for up to a week.

## Equipment Hack

Use 6 mini muffin tin liners instead.

## Tip

For a flavor twist, substitute butterscotch chips for the white chocolate.

# Rocky Road Fudge

**Makes 6 pieces of fudge** • **Prep time: 5 minutes, plus 2 hours to chill** •
**Mini Equipment, No-Bake**

This is a smooth dark chocolate fudge studded with crunchy nuts and pillowy sweet marshmallows. It's easier to make than a traditional fudge, and you don't even need a candy thermometer.

Unsalted butter, at room temperature, for preparing the loaf pan

3 ounces semisweet chocolate, finely chopped

2 teaspoons unsalted butter

¼ cup plus 3 tablespoons sweetened condensed milk

⅛ teaspoon vanilla extract

⅓ cup mini marshmallows

¼ cup chopped walnuts

1. **Prepare the pan.** Line your dessert vessel(s) with aluminum foil and then butter the foil (or skip the foil and just butter the pan).

2. **Make the fudge mixture.** In a medium microwave-safe bowl, combine the chocolate and butter. Microwave in 30-second intervals, stirring in between, until the chocolate is completely melted and the mixture is smooth. Add the condensed milk and vanilla and stir to incorporate. Stir in the marshmallows and walnuts. Spread the mixture in an even layer in the prepared dessert vessel(s).

3. **Chill and serve.** Chill in the refrigerator for at least 2 hours, until completely set. To serve, let the fudge come to room temperature, then slice it into squares. Store in an airtight container at room temperature for up to a week.

## Equipment Hack

Use 8 wells of a muffin tin or 8 mini muffin foil liners in a regular tin instead.

## Tip

To easily line the pan with foil and keep the foil mostly smooth, form the foil over the outside of the inverted pan. Flip the pan over and insert the foil liner. Use a large enough piece of foil so there is overhang to make it easy to lift the fudge out of the pan.

# Peppermint Chocolate Bark

**Makes 4 pieces** • **Prep time: 10 minutes, plus 50 minutes to chill** •
**Cook time: 6 to 8 minutes**

This irresistible peppermint bark includes layers of dark chocolate, peppermint-infused white chocolate, and crunchy crushed-up candy canes. It's an easy dessert that's perfect around the holidays, and also makes a great gift.

2 ounces semisweet chocolate, finely chopped, or 2 ounces semisweet chocolate chips

2 ounces white chocolate, finely chopped

⅛ teaspoon peppermint extract (optional)

¼ cup crushed peppermint candies or candy canes (about 2 candy canes)

1. ***Make the dark chocolate layer.*** Line a baking sheet with parchment paper. Spread the semisweet chocolate in a single layer on the prepared sheet. Spread it so there isn't much space between the chocolate pieces (it won't cover the whole pan). Place the baking sheet in the oven, then turn the oven on to 350°F. Bake for 6 to 8 minutes, until the chocolate is soft and mostly melted. Use a knife or a rubber spatula to spread the chocolate around so that it melts completely and is in an even layer. Refrigerate for about 20 minutes, until set.

2. ***Make the white chocolate layer.*** In a double boiler (or a metal bowl over a saucepan with about an inch of water in it), melt the white chocolate over simmering water, stirring frequently, about 5 minutes. Once completely melted, stir in the peppermint extract (if using).

3. ***Assemble the bark.*** Pour the melted white chocolate over the top of the set semisweet chocolate layer and spread it into an even layer. Immediately sprinkle the crushed peppermints over the top. Refrigerate for another 30 minutes or so, until the white chocolate layer is completely set. Break the bark into pieces. Serve immediately or store in an airtight container at room temperature.

## Tip

You can crush the candy canes either by putting them in a resealable plastic bag and smashing them with a rolling pin or by whizzing them in a blender or food processor.

# Dark Chocolate Cherry Almond Bark

**Makes 4 pieces • Prep time: 5 minutes, plus 30 minutes to chill • Cook time: 8 minutes**

Chocolate bark is easy to make—it's just a matter of melting chocolate and sprinkling other ingredients on top. The fun is in getting creative with your toppings and making your own custom-designed candy bars. Any type of nut or dried fruit is bound to be a good addition, as are shredded coconut, bits of crushed candy canes, and crunchy cereals or broken cookie bits.

4 ounces semisweet chocolate, finely chopped (or use 4 ounces semisweet chocolate chips)

⅓ cup toasted sliced almonds

¼ cup chopped dried cherries

1. **Make the bark.** Line a baking sheet with parchment paper. Spread the semisweet chocolate in a single layer on the prepared sheet. Spread it so there isn't much space between the chocolate pieces (it won't cover the whole pan). Place the baking sheet in the oven, then turn the oven on to 350°F. Bake for 6 to 8 minutes, until the chocolate is soft and mostly melted. Use a knife or a rubber spatula to spread the chocolate around so that it melts completely and is in an even layer. Immediately sprinkle the almonds and cherries over the top.

2. **Chill and serve.** Refrigerate for about 30 minutes, until the chocolate is set. Break the bark into pieces. Serve immediately or store in an airtight container at room temperature.

## Tip

To toast whole almonds, spread them in a single layer on a baking sheet. Toast in a preheated 350°F oven for 10 to 15 minutes, or until golden. To remove the skins, wrap the hot nuts in a clean kitchen towel and let them sit for a minute or two to steam, then use the towel to rub the skins off.

# Pecan Brittle

**Makes 4 pieces • Prep time: 5 minutes, plus 30 minutes to cool •
Cook time: 8 minutes • No-Bake**

Pecan brittle is as easy to make as chocolate bark, especially if you use the microwave to melt the sugar. You can substitute any other nuts for the pecans (peanuts, walnuts, almonds, or cashews, for example). If you have any leftover brittle, try crushing it up and stirring it into your next batch of homemade ice cream, or use it as a sundae topping.

Unsalted butter, at room
 temperature, for greasing
 the pan
½ cup granulated sugar

¼ cup light corn syrup
¾ cup toasted pecan halves
2 tablespoons unsalted butter
2 tablespoons water

½ teaspoon baking soda
¾ teaspoon vanilla extract

1. **Prepare the pan.** Grease the baking pan or baking sheet with butter.

2. **Make the brittle.** In a medium microwave-safe bowl, stir together the sugar and corn syrup. Microwave on high for 4 minutes. Stir in the pecans and microwave for another 4 minutes. Add the butter, water, baking soda, and vanilla and stir to mix. The very hot mixture will bubble up when you add the baking soda, so be careful.

3. **Spread and cool the brittle.** Pour the brittle mixture into the prepared pan. Use the back of a metal spoon to spread it out to about ¼-inch thickness. Let cool completely at room temperature, about 30 minutes. Break the brittle into pieces for serving. Store in an airtight container at room temperature for up to 2 weeks.

## Equipment Hack

Use a baking sheet instead.

## Tip

Toast the pecans on a parchment-lined baking sheet in a 350°F oven, stirring once or twice, for 5 to 7 minutes.

# 7
# PUDDINGS, CUSTARDS, AND CRÈMES

Banana and Butterscotch
Pudding Parfaits

**PAGE 154**

*C*ustards and puddings are often what we think of as old-fashioned comfort food desserts, but they can also be modern, sophisticated creations. Either way, they are smooth, creamy, and luscious little pots or bowls of joy. From Berries in Coconut Cream to Orange Panna Cotta to Salted Caramel Pots de Crème, these decadent desserts are perfect for making in individual servings. Custards are usually thickened with egg yolks, but you can use the whites for Chocolate Soufflés, or check the index on page 189 for other ideas for using spare egg whites.

Berries in Coconut Cream **144**

Strawberry Mousse **145**

Whipped Lemon Ricotta Mousse **146**

Chocolate Soufflés **147**

Blackberry Vanilla Bread Pudding **149**

Butterscotch Bread Pudding **150**

Coconut Rice Pudding with Fresh Mangos **151**

Espresso Custard **152**

Orange Panna Cotta **153**

Banana and Butterscotch Pudding Parfaits **154**

Caramel Apple Yogurt Parfaits **155**

Maple Pecan Tapioca Pudding **156**

Dark Chocolate Pudding **157**

Salted Caramel Pots de Crème **158**

Pumpkin Flan **159**

Strawberry Clafoutis **161**

Coffee-Poached Pears with Caramel Syrup **162**

Mixed Berry Summer Pudding **163**

# Berries in Coconut Cream

**Makes 2 servings • Prep time: 10 minutes, plus 1 hour to chill • Lightly Sweet, No-Bake**

Whipped coconut cream is one of my favorite things. Regular whipped cream is delicious, of course, but the additional flavor of coconut only adds to the appeal in my opinion. But the best thing is that you can keep a can of coconut milk in your refrigerator for months and you'll always be able to whip up a sweet, fluffy dream bowl whenever the craving strikes. Add fresh summer berries and you've got yourself a stellar dessert.

1 (14-ounce) unopened can full-fat coconut milk, refrigerated for at least 24 hours (I refrigerate the can upside down)

1 tablespoon confectioners' sugar, plus additional if desired

½ teaspoon vanilla extract

1 cup fresh berries (blackberries, blueberries, raspberries, strawberries, or a combination)

1. **Whip the coconut cream.** Take the chilled coconut milk out of the refrigerator and flip it over (if you've stored the can upside down, flip it to right-side up). This is so the thin liquid is at the top of the can. Open the can and pour off the thin liquid (pour it into a jar or other airtight container and save it for another use). The solid cream will be left in the can; place this in a medium bowl. Using an electric mixer fitted with the whisk attachment, beat the coconut cream on high until fluffy, 3 to 5 minutes. Add the confectioners' sugar and the vanilla and beat to incorporate. Taste and add additional sugar, if desired. Refrigerate the whipped cream until you are ready to assemble the dessert.

2. **Assemble and serve.** Bring the whipped cream to room temperature and re-whip if necessary. Add a layer of cream in the dessert vessels, then a layer of fresh berries. Continue layering until you've used all the cream, ending with a layer of berries. Serve immediately.

## Equipment Hack

Use two short, wide glasses instead of canning jars.

## Tip

Save the thin coconut milk liquid and add it to smoothies or use it to make ice cubes that can be added to water or iced coffee for extra flavor.

# Strawberry Mousse

EQUIPMENT/TOOLS: METAL OR GLASS BOWL, BLENDER OR FOOD PROCESSOR,
ELECTRIC MIXER, TWO 8-OUNCE CANNING JARS, PLASTIC WRAP

**Makes 2 servings • Prep time: 10 minutes, plus 1 hour to chill • No-Bake**

Fluffy, creamy mousse with juicy fresh strawberries is a great dessert for Valentine's Day, an anniversary, or your loved one's birthday, but it works any time of year for me. I use only strawberries, sugar, and cream in this version. A traditional mousse also includes egg whites, but I left them out here. The whipped cream is plenty light and delightfully rich.

¼ pound fresh strawberries, hulled and sliced, plus 2 whole strawberries for garnish

¼ cup granulated sugar

½ cup heavy (whipping) cream

1. ***Chill a bowl and purée the strawberries.*** Chill a metal or glass bowl in the freezer for 30 minutes. In a blender or food processor, combine the sliced strawberries and sugar and purée until smooth.

2. ***Make the mousse.*** Pour the cream into the chilled bowl. Using an electric mixer on high, beat the cream until it forms stiff peaks. Add the strawberry purée. Using a rubber spatula, gently fold in the purée into the cream until well combined. Spoon the mousse into your serving vessels and cover with plastic wrap. Refrigerate for at least an hour or overnight.

3. ***Serve.*** Slice the remaining strawberries and arrange the slices on top of the mousse as a garnish. Serve immediately.

## Equipment Hack

Use two short, wide glasses instead of canning jars.

## Tip

If strawberries aren't in season, you can substitute frozen ones. Thaw them at room temperature on a paper towel–lined plate. The paper towel will absorb the excess water the strawberries will release as they defrost.

# Whipped Lemon Ricotta Mousse

**EQUIPMENT/TOOLS: FOOD PROCESSOR, TWO 6-OUNCE RAMEKINS, PLASTIC WRAP**

**Makes 2 servings · Prep time: 5 minutes, plus 1 hour to chill · No-Bake**

This is one of those impressive desserts that is ridiculously easy to make, but tastes impossibly rich. I've flavored it with tart lemon zest and juice, but you can play around with all sorts of other flavors yourself. You'll get the smoothest texture by using a food processor, but you can make it in a blender or stand mixer, or even stir it together by hand.

¾ cup plus 2 tablespoons whole-milk ricotta cheese

¼ cup confectioners' sugar

¼ cup heavy (whipping) cream

1 teaspoon grated lemon zest

1 tablespoon freshly squeezed lemon juice

¼ teaspoon vanilla extract

1. **Make the mousse.** In a food processor, combine the ricotta, confectioners' sugar, cream, lemon zest and juice, and vanilla and process until smooth. Spoon the mousse into your serving vessels.

2. **Chill and serve.** Cover the vessels with plastic wrap and chill in the refrigerator for at least 1 hour. Serve chilled.

## Equipment Hack

Use two 8-ounce canning jars or short, wide glasses instead.

## Tip

For a chocolate ricotta mousse, omit the lemon zest and juice and add 2 tablespoons of unsweetened cocoa powder.

# Chocolate Soufflés

**Makes 2 soufflés • Prep time: 10 minutes • Cook time: 20 minutes • Quick**

Soufflés are the height of sophistication when it comes to dessert. It's a commonly held belief that they are super finicky to make, but they're actually quite simple. The only real trick is to be very gentle when folding the egg whites into the chocolate mixture so that you maintain all the airiness you've whipped into the egg whites since that's what makes a soufflé rise. You also want to serve them right when they come out of the oven before they begin to fall.

| | | |
|---|---|---|
| 3 tablespoons unsalted butter, divided | ½ teaspoon vanilla extract | Pinch kosher salt |
| 2 tablespoons unsweetened cocoa powder | 2 large eggs, yolks and whites separated | Pinch cream of tartar |
| 3 ounces semisweet chocolate, finely chopped | 2 tablespoons granulated sugar | Confectioners' sugar, for garnish |

1. **Preheat the oven and prepare the ramekins.** Preheat the oven to 375°F. Grease the serving vessels with 1 tablespoon of the butter. Sprinkle the cocoa powder into the ramekins, shake it around to coat, and then tap out the excess.

2. **Make the chocolate mixture.** In a double boiler or a large bowl set over a saucepan with 1 inch of simmering water, add the chocolate and the remaining 2 tablespoons of butter. Heat the chocolate, stirring occasionally, until smooth. Remove from the heat and stir in the vanilla. Add the egg yolks, one at a time, whisking after each addition until smooth.

3. **Make the egg white mixture.** In a large bowl, combine the egg whites, sugar, salt, and cream of tartar and use an electric mixer on high to beat until stiff peaks form.

➤

4. ***Assemble the soufflés.*** Using a rubber spatula, gently fold the egg white mixture into the chocolate mixture. Divide this between the prepared vessels. Set the vessels on a baking sheet (to make it easy to put them in and take them out of the oven).

5. ***Bake and serve.*** Bake for about 20 minutes, until the soufflés puff up. Serve immediately, garnished with a dusting of confectioners' sugar.

## Tip

You can make the soufflés through step 4 and refrigerate them, covered with plastic wrap, for up to 24 hours.

# *Blackberry Vanilla Bread Pudding*

EQUIPMENT/TOOLS: MINI LOAF PAN, NONSTICK COOKING SPRAY

**Makes 2 servings · Prep time: 10 minutes · Cook: 30 to 35 minutes · Mini Equipment**

Bread pudding is a classic dessert, the kind of comforting bowl of love that Grandma used to make. This version features juicy blackberries and a vanilla-scented custard that is to die for.

2 cups cubed bread (choose an egg bread like challah or brioche for best results)

½ cup fresh blackberries

1 large egg

½ cup whole milk

2 tablespoons sugar

½ teaspoon vanilla extract

Whipped cream, for serving (optional)

1. ***Preheat the oven and prepare the pan.*** Preheat the oven to 350°F. Grease your baking vessel(s) with nonstick cooking spray.

2. ***Assemble the bread pudding.*** Layer the bread cubes and blackberries in the pan. Start with a layer of bread, then add a layer of blackberries, another layer of bread, another layer of blackberries, and finish with the rest of the bread.

3. ***Make the custard.*** In a medium bowl, combine the egg, milk, sugar, and vanilla and whisk to combine thoroughly. Pour this over the bread and blackberries, being sure all of the bread pieces are soaked with the custard.

4. ***Bake and serve.*** Bake for 30 to 35 minutes, until the top is golden brown and the pudding is cooked through. Let cool for 15 to 20 minutes before serving. Serve warm, garnished with a dollop of whipped cream (if using).

## *Equipment Hack*

Use two wells of a muffin tin instead.

## *Tip*

For added texture and flavor, add a streusel topping to the bread pudding. Combine 1 tablespoon flour, 1 tablespoon brown sugar, 1 tablespoon cold, unsalted butter, and 1 tablespoon chopped nuts and sprinkle over the top of the puddings before baking.

# Butterscotch Bread Pudding

EQUIPMENT/TOOLS: TWO 8-OUNCE RAMEKINS, NONSTICK COOKING SPRAY, SAUCEPAN

**Makes 2 servings • Prep time: 10 minutes • Cook time: 45 minutes**

I cannot get enough butterscotch. There is just something about that caramelly, cooked brown sugar flavor that just hits my pleasure center. It gets bonus points by being even easier to make than a traditional caramel. Here it flavors a simple bread pudding, making it taste truly extravagant.

2 tablespoons water

¼ cup brown sugar

2 tablespoons unsalted butter

½ cup heavy (whipping) cream

½ cup whole milk

1 large egg

½ teaspoon vanilla extract

1½ cups cubed bread (choose a mild-flavored bread or an egg bread like challah or brioche for best results)

1. **Preheat the oven and prepare the pan.** Preheat the oven to 350°F. Grease the baking vessels with nonstick cooking spray.

2. **Make the custard.** In a small saucepan over high heat, combine the water and sugar. Heat, without stirring, until the sugar dissolves and the mixture cooks down to a syrupy consistency. As soon as the mixture begins to turn golden brown, begin swirling the pan. Continue to cook until the mixture is a deep golden brown color, 6 to 8 minutes. Whisk in the butter. Remove the pan from the heat and whisk in the cream. Whisk in the milk, egg, and vanilla.

3. **Assemble the bread puddings.** Add the bread cubes to the custard mixture and let them absorb the liquid. Divide the bread between the two prepared vessels and then pour any remaining liquid over the top.

4. **Bake and serve.** Bake for 35 to 40 minutes, until the tops are golden brown and the puddings are cooked through. Let cool for 15 to 20 minutes before serving. Serve warm.

## Tip

For the best bread pudding, use stale bread. If you don't have stale bread, toast your bread cubes in a 250°F oven for 10 minutes or so to dry it out.

# *Coconut Rice Pudding with Fresh Mangos*

**Makes 2 servings • Prep time: 10 minutes • Cook time: 45 minutes • No-Bake**

Using just a handful of ingredients and a single pot, this tropical-flavored pudding is one of my favorites. Delicate jasmine rice is simmered in rich coconut milk until the mixture is thick and creamy. A topping of sweet, juicy mango cuts the richness of the coconut milk.

¼ cup full-fat coconut milk

¼ cup granulated sugar

½ teaspoon vanilla extract

¼ teaspoon kosher salt

1½ cups cooked jasmine rice (about ½ cup raw rice cooked according to package directions)

1 large, ripe mango, peeled and sliced

1. **Make the cooking liquid.** In a medium saucepan over medium-low heat, whisk together the coconut milk, sugar, vanilla, and salt. Cook, stirring frequently and being careful not to let the mixture come to a boil, until the sugar is dissolved, about 5 minutes.

2. **Add the rice.** Add the cooked rice and stir to mix well. Cover the pot and reduce the heat to low. Let simmer for 15 to 20 minutes, until the rice has absorbed most of the liquid.

3. **Garnish and serve.** Spoon the rice pudding into two small serving bowls. Top each with mango slices. Serve warm.

## *Tip*

For a dramatic look and extra nutrients, substitute forbidden black rice for the jasmine rice.

# Espresso Custard

EQUIPMENT/TOOLS: TWO 8-OUNCE RAMEKINS OR CANNING JARS,
SKILLET OR LARGE SAUCEPAN, PLASTIC WRAP

**Makes 2 custards • Prep time: 5 minutes, plus 4 hours to chill •
Cook time: 10 minutes • Lightly Sweet**

This dessert is like a refreshing, lightly sweetened iced coffee in custard form, and will give you a welcome lift. It's smooth, creamy, and just sweet enough, and it delivers a hearty kick of espresso flavor. It makes a perfect ending to any meal.

1½ cups milk

1 large egg yolk

1 large egg

2 tablespoons
granulated sugar

1 tablespoon instant
espresso powder

¾ teaspoon vanilla extract

1. *Make the custard.* In a medium bowl, whisk together the milk, egg yolk, egg, sugar, espresso powder, and vanilla. Spoon the custard into your serving vessels.

2. *Steam and chill.* On the stove top, set the ramekins in a skillet or saucepan with water that comes three-quarters of the way up the sides of the ramekins. Turn the heat to high until the water comes to a boil, then reduce the heat to low, cover the pan, and simmer for 10 minutes. Using tongs, remove the vessels from the pan and cover with plastic wrap. Chill in the refrigerator for at least 4 hours. Serve chilled.

## Tip

Serve a couple of crisp cookies along with this creamy custard for a delightful textural contrast.

# *Orange Panna Cotta*

**EQUIPMENT/TOOLS: SAUCEPAN, TWO 8-OUNCE RAMEKINS OR
CANNING JARS, PLASTIC WRAP**

**Makes 2 panna cotta • Prep time: 5 minutes, plus 4 hours to chill •
Cook time: 10 minutes • Lightly Sweet, No-Bake**

Easy and quick to make, perfectly creamy and with a luscious smoothness, panna cotta is a lovely dessert that is easy to switch up to accommodate both flavor preferences and dietary considerations. This version uses orange zest to infuse the milk base with citrusy flavor.

| | | |
|---|---|---|
| 1 teaspoon powdered gelatin | 1⅓ cups whole milk | 2 strips fresh orange peel |
| 1 tablespoon water | ¼ cup granulated sugar | (orange part only) |
| | | ½ teaspoon vanilla extract |

1. ***Soften the gelatin.*** In a small bowl, sprinkle the gelatin over the water. Do not sir. Let soak 10 minutes.

2. ***Make the panna cotta.*** In a small saucepan over low heat, stir together the milk, sugar, and orange peel and cook, stirring occasionally, until the sugar dissolves, about 5 minutes. Raise the heat to medium and continue to cook, stirring frequently, for 5 minutes more. Remove the pan from the heat and immediately stir in the gelatin and the vanilla. Stir until the gelatin dissolves. Let cool for 5 minutes. Remove the orange peel.

3. ***Chill the panna cotta.*** Divide the panna cotta between the serving vessels. Cover with plastic wrap and chill in the refrigerator for at least 4 hours. Serve chilled.

## *Tip*

Make this a vegan dessert by substituting a vegetarian gelatin, like agar agar, and use soy, coconut, or almond milk for the cow's milk.

# Banana and Butterscotch Pudding Parfaits

EQUIPMENT/TOOLS: SAUCEPAN, PLASTIC WRAP, TWO 8-OUNCE
CANNING JARS OR GLASSES

**Makes 2 parfaits • Prep time: 20 minutes, plus 2 hours to chill •
Cook time: 10 minutes • No-Bake**

The buttery sweetness of caramelized brown sugar mingles delightfully with bananas in this refreshingly simple pudding parfait. The crumbled gingersnaps add a welcome crunch, as well as a hint of spice that counters the richness of the custard.

1 cup whole milk

2 large egg yolks

½ cup brown sugar

1½ tablespoons cornstarch

⅛ teaspoon kosher salt

2 teaspoons unsalted butter

2 bananas, sliced

4 to 6 Spicy Ginger Cookies (page 28) or store-bought gingersnaps, crumbled

1. **Make the pudding.** In a medium bowl, whisk together the milk and egg yolks. In a medium saucepan, whisk together the brown sugar, cornstarch, and salt. Add the egg yolk mixture and whisk to combine. Place the pan over medium heat and cook, stirring occasionally, until the mixture begins to bubble and thicken, about 10 minutes. When the mixture is very thick, add the butter and stir until it is completely melted. Transfer the pudding to a bowl, cover with plastic wrap, and chill in the refrigerator for at least 2 hours.

2. **Assemble the parfaits.** Place a large spoonful of pudding in the bottom of each serving vessel. Top with one-third of the banana slices and one-third of the cookie crumbs. Repeat with two more layers each of pudding, banana, and cookie crumbs. Serve immediately or refrigerate until ready to serve.

# *Caramel Apple Yogurt Parfaits*

**EQUIPMENT/TOOLS: SAUCEPAN, TWO 8-OUNCE CANNING JARS OR GLASSES**

**Makes 2 parfaits • Prep time: 10 minutes • Cook time: 10 minutes • Quick, No-Bake**

I've always loved the idea of caramel apples—the two flavors are practically made for each other—but biting into a whole apple that's been dunked in sticky caramel is daunting. This pretty dessert combines those flavors in an easy-to-devour parfait.

**FOR THE CARAMEL SAUCE**

2 tablespoons unsalted butter

¼ cup plus 2 tablespoons light brown sugar

¼ cup heavy (whipping) cream

Pinch kosher salt

¾ teaspoon vanilla extract

**FOR THE PARFAITS**

1½ cups plain yogurt

1 apple, cored and diced

1 tablespoon chopped toasted pecans

1. **Make the caramel sauce.** In a medium saucepan over low heat, stir together the butter, brown sugar, cream, and salt until the mixture is smooth and the sugar dissolved. Raise the heat to medium and bring to a boil. Let the mixture boil, undisturbed, for 10 minutes, reducing the heat as needed to prevent it from burning. Remove the pan from the heat and gently stir in the vanilla. Let cool for 15 to 20 minutes.

2. **Assemble the parfaits.** Spoon ¼ cup of yogurt into the bottom of each serving vessel. Add one-quarter of the apple in on top of the yogurt, then spoon a tablespoon of caramel sauce over the apples. Top with another layer of yogurt, apples, and caramel sauce, and finish with a layer of yogurt and a drizzle of the sauce. Garnish with a sprinkle of pecans on top. Serve immediately.

## *Tip*

If you don't want to make your own caramel sauce, you can always substitute a store-bought jarred version.

# Maple Pecan Tapioca Pudding

EQUIPMENT/TOOLS: SAUCEPAN, TWO 8-OUNCE RAMEKINS OR CANNING JARS,
PLASTIC WRAP, BAKING SHEET, PARCHMENT PAPER

Makes 2 puddings • Prep time: 5 minutes, plus 2 hours to chill •
Cook time: 10 minutes • No-Bake

Tapioca pudding is a simple, timeless dessert and this version, flavored with maple syrup and pecans, is a standout. I use the smaller, quick-cooking tapioca pearls because they don't need to be presoaked. The pudding still needs to chill for a couple of hours before serving, but the actual prep and cooking time is just 15 minutes.

| | | |
|---|---|---|
| 1 cup milk | Pinch kosher salt | 2 tablespoons |
| 1 large egg | ¼ cup plus 1 tablespoon maple | chopped pecans |
| 2 tablespoons | syrup, divided | |
| quick-cooking tapioca | ¼ teaspoon of vanilla extract | |

1. **Make the pudding.** In a medium saucepan, stir together the milk, egg, tapioca, and salt. Let stand for 5 minutes to soak the tapioca. Place the pan over medium-low heat and bring the mixture just to a boil, stirring frequently. Remove the pan from the heat and stir in ¼ cup of maple syrup and the vanilla. Divide the pudding between the serving vessels. Cover with plastic wrap and refrigerate for at least 2 hours.

2. **Make the maple pecans.** Line a baking sheet with parchment paper. In a small saucepan over medium heat, toss the pecans with the remaining tablespoon of maple syrup. Cook, stirring frequently, until the liquid has mostly evaporated, 3 to 4 minutes. Spread the nuts out on the prepared baking sheet. Chill in the refrigerator or freezer until hardened.

3. **Garnish and serve.** Serve the chilled pudding topped with the maple pecans.

## Tip

If you prefer to use the non-quick-cooking tapioca pearls, you'll need to soak them before cooking. Use 2 tablespoons and soak them in ½ cup of water for 30 minutes, then drain. Make the recipe as directed, except skip the step where the tapioca pearls, milk, egg, and salt stand for 5 minutes and just start cooking.

# Dark Chocolate Pudding

**Makes 2 puddings • Prep time: 10 minutes, plus 2 hours to chill •
Cook time: 10 minutes • No-Bake**

Pudding differs from custard in that it is thickened with starch, while custard gets its sturdy texture from egg yolks. Use a good-quality dark chocolate for this classic pudding to have the richest chocolate flavor. Cooked with whole milk and cornstarch, it turns into a decadent bowl of creamy goodness.

¼ cup granulated sugar

2 tablespoons cornstarch

⅛ teaspoon kosher salt

1½ cups whole milk

3 ounces semisweet chocolate, finely chopped

½ teaspoon vanilla extract

Whipped cream, for serving (optional)

1. ***Make the pudding.*** In a small saucepan, combine the sugar, cornstarch, and salt. Set the pan over medium-low heat and whisk in the milk until smooth. Cook, reducing the heat as needed to prevent the mixture from boiling, whisking occasionally, until the mixture thickens, about 10 minutes. Whisk in the chocolate until it is completely melted and the mixture is smooth. Remove the pan from the heat and stir in the vanilla.

2. ***Strain and chill.*** Strain the pudding through a fine-mesh strainer into your serving vessels. Cover with plastic wrap, pressing it down to sit on the surface of the pudding. Chill in the refrigerator for at least 2 hours.

3. ***Serve.*** Serve the chilled pudding topped with a dollop of whipped cream (if using).

# Salted Caramel Pots de Crème

EQUIPMENT/TOOLS: SAUCEPAN, TWO 6-OUNCE RAMEKINS OR CANNING JARS,
BAKING DISH, ALUMINUM FOIL, WIRE RACK, PLASTIC WRAP

**Makes 2 pots de crème • Prep time: 10 minutes, plus 2 hours to chill •
Cook time: 40 minutes**

This classic custard, flavored with brown sugar caramel, gets a modern twist with the addition of a flaky sea salt garnish. The salt adds a welcome crunch, and it balances out the sweetness of the caramel. With just 10 minutes of prep, this creamy dessert is a treasure.

| | | |
|---|---|---|
| 2 tablespoons unsalted butter | ⅓ cup heavy (whipping) cream | ¾ teaspoon vanilla extract |
| ½ cup light brown sugar | ⅓ cup whole milk | Flaky sea salt, for serving |
| ⅛ teaspoon kosher salt | 1 large egg yolk | |

1. **Preheat the oven and make the custard.** Preheat the oven to 325°F. In a small saucepan over medium heat, melt the butter. Whisk in the brown sugar and salt, then add the cream and milk. Continue to heat, whisking occasionally, until the mixture is very hot but not boiling, about 5 minutes. Reduce the heat as needed to prevent boiling. In a medium bowl, beat the egg yolk. While whisking constantly, slowly drizzle the milk mixture into the yolk in a thin stream. Stir in the vanilla.

2. **Bake the custards.** Divide the custard between your serving vessels. Fill a small baking dish with about an inch of boiling water. Place the vessels in the water bath. Loosely cover the dish with aluminum foil. Bake until the custard is set, about 35 minutes. Transfer the custards to a wire rack to cool for 15 minutes. Cover the custards with plastic wrap, pressing it down to sit on the surface of the custard. Chill in the refrigerator for at least 2 hours.

3. **Garnish and serve.** Serve the chilled pots de crème, sprinkled with the flaky sea salt.

## Tip

You can use any coarse-grained sea salt to garnish your pots de crème, but I like to use Maldon sea salt because its delicate pyramid-shaped flakes give it a nice crunchy, light texture. Other good options include *fleur de sel* and *sel gris*.

# Pumpkin Flan

**EQUIPMENT/TOOLS: SAUCEPAN, TWO 6-OUNCE RAMEKINS OR CANNING JARS, FINE-MESH STRAINER, BAKING DISH, WIRE RACK, PLASTIC WRAP**

**Makes 2 flans • Prep time: 10 minutes, plus 8 hours to chill • Cook time: 40 minutes**

My mother has always been famous for her flan. When I was growing up, I believed she was some kind of kitchen magician because her flan always turned out so beautifully. It turns out that flan is actually deceptively simple to make. This pumpkin-flavored version, made in individual-size portions, is every bit as magical as my mother's.

**FOR THE CARAMEL**

¼ cup plus 3 tablespoons granulated sugar, divided

**FOR THE CUSTARD**

1 large egg

1 large egg yolk

½ cup whole milk

2 tablespoons heavy (whipping) cream

⅓ cup pumpkin purée

½ teaspoon pumpkin pie spice

¼ teaspoon vanilla extract

1. ***Preheat the oven and make the caramel.*** Preheat the oven to 325°F. Place 3 tablespoons of sugar in a small saucepan. Heat over medium heat until the sugar begins to melt. Tilt and swirl the pan over the heat until the sugar turns golden brown, about 5 minutes. Immediately pour the hot caramel into your serving cooking vessels. Swirl and tilt the vessels so the caramel evenly coats the bottoms before it hardens.

2. ***Make the custard.*** In a medium bowl, whisk together the egg, egg yolk, milk, cream, pumpkin purée, pumpkin pie spice, vanilla, and the remaining ¼ cup of sugar until smooth. Strain the custard through a fine-mesh sieve on top of the caramel. Place the vessels in a baking dish and pour in enough hot water around the vessels so it comes about halfway up the sides of the vessels.

➤

3. ***Bake the custard.*** Bake for about 35 minutes, until the edges are set and there is still just a bit of jiggle in the center. Transfer the vessels to a wire rack and let stand for 15 minutes. Cover the ramekins with plastic wrap and chill in the refrigerator for at least 8 hours.

4. ***Serve.*** Run a knife around the edge of the chilled flan to loosen it from the sides of the vessel. Invert the flan onto a serving plate, leaving the vessel in place. Let the vessel sit on the plate upside down for several minutes before lifting it off. The caramel should flow over the custard. Serve immediately.

## Tip

For a silky smooth custard texture, be careful not to whisk a lot of air or bubbles into the custard mixture. Whisk thoroughly but gently to combine without creating bubbles.

# Strawberry Clafoutis

**Makes 2 servings • Prep time: 10 minutes • Cook time: 20 minutes • Quick, Lightly Sweet**

I love to make clafoutis for guests. It sounds super fancy, but is really simple to make. It starts with a layer of fruit that's bathed in a lightly sweetened batter that cooks up like a cross between a dense cake and a rich custard.

Unsalted butter, at room temperature, for preparing the ramekins

1 tablespoon unsalted butter, melted

¼ cup plus 2 tablespoons whole milk

¼ cup all-purpose flour

3 tablespoons sugar

1 large egg

Pinch kosher salt

1 cup diced fresh strawberries

Confectioners' sugar, for serving (optional)

1. **Preheat the oven and prepare the ramekins.** Preheat the oven to 350°F. Grease the ramekins with the butter.

2. **Make the batter.** In a medium bowl or a blender, combine the butter, milk, flour, sugar, egg, and salt and whisk or blend until smooth.

3. **Assemble the clafoutis.** Divide the strawberries between the two prepared ramekins. Pour the batter over the fruit.

4. **Bake and serve.** Bake about 20 minutes, until the batter is set and golden brown on top. Place the ramekins on a wire rack to cool for a few minutes before sprinkling with confectioners' sugar (if using). Serve warm or at room temperature.

# Coffee-Poached Pears with Caramel Syrup

**Makes 2 servings • Prep time: 5 minutes • Cook time: 18 minutes • Quick, No-Bake**

Poaching pears in brown sugar-sweetened coffee infuses the sweet fruit with the unexpected but delightfully rich flavor of coffee. A slight hint of bitterness balances out the sweetness of the caramel syrup. Toasted hazelnuts add crunch.

1 cup water

1 tablespoon freshly squeezed lemon juice

⅓ cup plus 1 tablespoon granulated sugar, divided

½ cup brewed coffee

2 ripe pears, peeled, cored, and thinly sliced

½ teaspoon vanilla extract

2 tablespoons chopped toasted hazelnuts

1. ***Poach the pears.*** In a medium saucepan over high heat, combine the water, lemon juice, 1 tablespoon of the sugar, and the coffee and bring just to a boil. Reduce the heat to medium and add the pears. Simmer until the pears are tender, about 7 minutes.

2. ***Make the syrup.*** In a small saucepan over medium heat, heat the remaining ⅓ cup of sugar until it melts and turns deep golden brown, 4 to 6 minutes. Add ½ cup of the poaching liquid along with the vanilla. Simmer, stirring frequently, until the mixture has cooked down to a syrup, about 5 minutes.

3. ***Serve.*** Place the pears on serving plates and pour the syrup over them. Sprinkle the hazelnuts over the top. Serve warm.

## Tip

If you don't like coffee, you can use brewed tea instead. I love using Earl Grey because of its hint of citrusy bergamot oil.

# Mixed Berry Summer Pudding

**Makes 2 puddings • Prep time: 10 minutes, plus 6 hours to chill •
Cook time: 5 minutes • No-Bake, Lightly Sweet**

Summer pudding is a delightful warm weather dessert that's easy to make and looks stunning. Brightly colored berries are cooked to a juicy compote and then layered with soft, white sandwich bread. The bread absorbs the berry juices and the whole thing sets up thanks to the berries' natural pectin.

3 cups mixed fresh berries (any combination of sliced strawberries, blueberries, raspberries, blackberries, etc.)

2 tablespoons granulated sugar
2 tablespoons water
Pinch kosher salt

4 slices firm white sandwich bread, crusts trimmed off
2 tablespoons heavy (whipping) cream, for serving

1. **Make the berry compote.** In a medium saucepan over medium-high heat, stir together the berries, sugar, water, and salt and cook until the berries soften and break down, about 5 minutes. Scoop out about ⅓ cup of the berry mixture to use as a garnish, placing it in a bowl and refrigerating until ready to use.

2. **Assemble the puddings.** Trim the slices of bread into circles to fit inside the ramekins. Place a spoonful of the berry compote into each ramekin. Place one round of bread on top of the berries. Top this with the remaining berries. Place the remaining bread rounds on top.

3. **Chill the puddings.** Wrap each ramekin in plastic wrap and place them on a plate (to catch any overflowing juices). Place an unopened 15-ounce can (or another object of similar size/weight) on top of each of the puddings to weigh down the bread. Refrigerate for at least 6 hours.

4. **Plate and serve.** Remove the weight, unwrap the ramekins, and invert the ramekins onto serving plates. Spoon the reserved berry compote on top and drizzle the cream over top. Serve immediately.

## *Tip*

You can make these puddings up to 2 days ahead. Keep them in their ramekins and store in the refrigerator, wrapped in plastic wrap. Store the berry garnish and the cream for drizzling separately and add just before serving.

# 8
# FROZEN TREATS

Very Berry Frozen
Yogurt Ice Pops

**PAGE 177**

**F**rozen desserts are always welcome when the weather turns warm, and you don't need to make large quantities or use fancy appliances. The recipes in this chapter range from easy ice creams and sorbets that don't require an ice cream maker to frozen ice pops and ice cream sandwiches that can be made two at a time. Try the Easy No-Churn Vanilla Ice Cream and get creative with add-ins to create your own unique flavors. Strawberry Balsamic Sorbet is simple to make, with a distinctive flavor from the balsamic vinegar. Cookies and Cream Ice Cream Cake is the perfect amount of celebration, especially for people who want a little bit of everything in their dessert!

Easy No-Churn Vanilla Ice Cream **166**

Grilled Peach Sundaes with Bourbon
    Caramel Sauce **167**

Hot Fudge Brownie Sundaes with Spiced
    Candied Pecans **169**

Strawberry Balsamic Sorbet **170**

Chocolate-Orange Sorbet **171**

Pink Grapefruit Granita **172**

Strawberry Champagne Granita **173**

Vietnamese Iced Coffee Float **174**

Crispy (Not) Fried Ice Cream **175**

Piña Colada Ice Pops **176**

Very Berry Frozen Yogurt Ice Pops **177**

Frozen Strawberry
    Cheesecake Pops **178**

Frozen Fudge Pops **179**

Classic Ice Cream Sandwiches **180**

Ginger-Lemon Ice Cream Cake **182**

Cookies and Cream Ice Cream Cake **183**

Frozen Raspberry Hot Chocolate **185**

# *Easy No-Churn Vanilla Ice Cream*

**Makes 2 scoops • Prep time: 10 minutes, plus 7 hours to chill and freeze • No-Bake**

Homemade ice cream is delicious, and you don't even need an ice cream maker to create this perennial favorite. This no-churn recipe takes 10 minutes to put together and then it's just about waiting for it to freeze. This simple vanilla version can be changed up easily by adding a few tablespoons of cookie crumbs (Oreos, gingersnaps, or any other cookie you love), nuts, swirls of fudge or caramel sauce, minced fruit, or spices like cinnamon or cardamom.

¼ cup sweetened condensed milk

½ teaspoon vanilla extract

½ cup cold heavy (whipping) cream

1. ***Chill the bowl.*** Place a medium stainless steel bowl in the freezer to chill for an hour.

2. ***Make the ice cream mixture.*** In a small bowl, stir together the sweetened condensed milk and vanilla. In a medium bowl, whip the cream with an electric mixer fitted with the whisk attachment on medium-high until stiff peaks form, about 2 minutes. Using a rubber spatula, scoop ¼ cup of the whipped cream into the bowl of condensed milk and fold them together until well combined. Add the lightened condensed milk mixture to the whipped cream and fold it in until well combined.

3. ***Freeze.*** Transfer the mixture to the chilled stainless steel bowl and cover with plastic wrap. Freeze for at least 6 hours, stirring the ice cream every 2 hours or so. Serve frozen.

## *Tip*

For extra creamy ice cream, add 1½ teaspoons of nonfat powdered milk to the cream before whipping it. This helps the whipped cream maintain its structure when it is folded into the sweetened condensed milk.

# Grilled Peach Sundaes with Bourbon Caramel Sauce

EQUIPMENT/TOOLS: SMALL SAUCEPAN

**Makes 2 sundaes • Prep time: 10 minutes • Cook time: 20 minutes • Quick, No-Bake**

Peaches and bourbon taste like warm, sultry summer nights. This simple dessert combines the two for a perfect finish to a barbecue or other backyard meal. The peaches caramelize on the grill, which enhances their sweetness and intensifies their flavor. A bourbon caramel sauce drizzled over the ice cream–filled grilled peach halves makes it downright decadent. Crunchy gingersnap crumbs are the cherry (so to speak) on top.

**FOR THE SAUCE**

¼ cup granulated sugar

1 tablespoon water

2 tablespoons heavy (whipping) cream

1 teaspoon bourbon

**FOR THE SUNDAES**

1 large, ripe peach, halved and pitted

1 tablespoon unsalted butter, melted

2 large scoops Easy No-Churn Vanilla Ice Cream (page 166) or store-bought ice cream

2 Spicy Ginger Cookies (page 28) or store-bought gingersnaps, crumbled

Whipped cream, for serving (optional)

2 tablespoons chopped toasted pecans

1. ***Make the sauce.*** In a small saucepan over medium heat, swirl the sugar and water together until the sugar is melted and the mixture turns a deep caramel color, about 15 minutes. Watch it carefully, reducing the heat if needed, as it can burn quickly. Remove the pan from the heat and slowly stir in the cream. Stir in the bourbon.

2. ***Preheat a grill and grill the peaches.*** Preheat a grill or grill pan to medium-high heat. Brush the cut side of the peach halves with the butter. Put the peaches on the grill, cut-side down, and grill until the peaches soften and have grill marks, about 5 minutes. Remove from the grill and let cool for a few minutes on a plate.

➤

3. ***Assemble the sundaes.*** Place the peaches cut-side up in 2 serving bowls. Top each peach half with a scoop of ice cream. Drizzle the bourbon sauce over the ice cream and then sprinkle with the cookie crumbs. Add a dollop of whipped cream (if using) and sprinkle the nuts over the top. Serve immediately.

## Tip

If grilling isn't an option, slice the peach and caramelize the slices in a sauté pan with butter and a bit of brown sugar.

# Hot Fudge Brownie Sundaes with Spiced Candied Pecans

EQUIPMENT/TOOLS: PARCHMENT PAPER, NONSTICK SKILLET

**Makes 2 sundaes • Prep time: 10 minutes • Cook time: 5 minutes • Quick, No-Bake**

A fudgy brownie topped with a scoop of cold, sweet vanilla ice cream, drizzled with rich, chocolatey hot fudge sauce, and finished with crunchy spiced and candied pecans makes a dessert to die for. The best part is that if you already have the brownies and ice cream, you can whip this up in 15 minutes.

**FOR THE HOT FUDGE SAUCE**
¼ cup heavy (whipping) cream
4 ounces semisweet chocolate, finely chopped
¼ teaspoon vanilla extract

**FOR THE CANDIED PECANS**
¼ cup pecans
1 tablespoon brown sugar
1 teaspoon unsalted butter
Pinch cinnamon

**FOR THE SUNDAES**
2 Classic Double Chocolate Brownies (page 39) or store-bought brownies
2 large scoops Easy No-Churn Vanilla Ice Cream (page 166) or store-bought ice cream

1. **Make the sauce.** In a medium microwave-safe bowl, combine the cream and chocolate. Microwave on high in 30-second intervals, stirring in between, until the chocolate is completely melted and the mixture is smooth. Stir in the vanilla.

2. **Make the candied pecans.** Line a plate with parchment paper. Warm a small nonstick skillet over medium heat. Heat the pecans, brown sugar, butter, and cinnamon, stirring constantly, until the sugar is completely dissolved and the nuts are fully coated, about 5 minutes. Transfer the nuts to the parchment paper and let cool. Once the mixture has hardened, break it apart with your hands.

3. **Assemble the sundaes.** Place one brownie on each of two dessert plates. Top each with a scoop of ice cream. Drizzle the hot fudge sauce over the ice cream and sprinkle the candied nuts over the top. Serve immediately.

## Tip

For a different presentation, break the brownies up into small squares and layer them in clear glasses with small scoops of ice cream (use a small cookie scoop) and then drizzle with the sauce and top with whipped cream and the candied pecans.

# Strawberry Balsamic Sorbet

**Makes 2 servings • Prep time: 10 minutes, plus 30 minutes to macerate the strawberries and 6 hours to freeze • Cook time: 2 minutes • No-Bake**

Sweet-tart balsamic vinegar works wonders on fresh strawberries, enhancing their natural sweetness, fruity flavor, and bright red hue. You can use a basic balsamic vinegar from the supermarket, but if you happen to have a fancy aged balsamic, use that instead. The concentrated sweetness of the syrupy aged version takes this sorbet over the top.

¼ pound fresh strawberries,
   hulled and quartered

1 tablespoon balsamic vinegar

¼ cup plus 1 teaspoon
   granulated sugar, divided

¼ cup water

1. ***Chill the bowl.*** Place a medium stainless steel bowl in the freezer for at least 1 hour.

2. ***Macerate the strawberries.*** In a small bowl, stir together the strawberries, vinegar, and 1 teaspoon of sugar. Set aside for 30 minutes to let the strawberries macerate.

3. ***Make a simple syrup.*** In a small saucepan over medium heat, heat the remaining ¼ cup of sugar and the water, stirring frequently, until the sugar fully dissolves. Remove the pan from the heat.

4. ***Purée the strawberries and freeze.*** Place the strawberries, along with any juice that has collected in the bowl, and the simple syrup in a blender and purée until smooth. Transfer the mixture to the chilled stainless steel bowl and cover with plastic wrap. Freeze for at least 6 hours, stirring every 2 hours. Serve frozen.

## Tip

This refreshing sorbet is fantastic on its own, but it's even better with a drizzle of hot fudge sauce (as most things are).

# Chocolate-Orange Sorbet

EQUIPMENT/TOOLS: STAINLESS STEEL BOWL, SAUCEPAN, PLASTIC WRAP

**Makes 2 servings • Prep time: 5 minutes, plus 6 hours to freeze •
Cook time: 5 minutes • No-Bake**

There was an ice cream shop in my hometown that made an amazing dark chocolate and orange ice cream that I was completely obsessed with when I was growing up. This sorbet captures that amazing flavor combination in a light, refreshing, and dairy-free sorbet.

¼ cup plus 2 tablespoons granulated sugar

⅔ cup plus 1½ tablespoons water

3½ ounces bittersweet chocolate, finely chopped

1 teaspoon finely grated orange zest

1 teaspoon unsweetened cocoa powder

1. ***Chill the bowl.*** Place a medium stainless steel bowl in the freezer for at least 1 hour.

2. ***Make the sorbet.*** In a small saucepan over medium heat, heat the sugar and water, stirring frequently, until the sugar has dissolved and the mixture thickens, about 5 minutes. In a medium bowl, combine the chocolate, orange zest, and cocoa powder. Pour the hot sugar water over the top and stir or whisk until the chocolate is completely melted and the mixture is smooth.

3. ***Freeze and serve.*** Place the sorbet in the stainless steel bowl and cover with plastic wrap. Freeze for at least 6 hours, stirring and breaking up the mixture with a fork every hour or so. Serve frozen.

## *Tip*

For a fun way to serve this sorbet, take 2 small oranges and cut off the tops. Scoop out the flesh (serve the segments alongside the sorbet if you like, or save for another use) and fill the orange peels with the sorbet. Garnish with a few fine strips of orange zest.

# Pink Grapefruit Granita

EQUIPMENT/TOOLS: SAUCEPAN, STAINLESS STEEL BOWL,
PLASTIC WRAP, TWO COCKTAIL GLASSES

**Makes 2 servings • Prep time: 5 minutes, plus 6 hours to freeze •
Cook time: 5 minutes • No-Bake, Lightly Sweet**

Granita is a refreshing frozen dessert of delicate ice crystals made with fresh fruit or fruit juice, water, and sugar. Blended, frozen, and broken up with a fork, it is a melt-in-your-mouth, fruit-flavored ice. It's like sorbet, only even easier to make.

| 2 tablespoons water | 2½ tablespoons granulated sugar | 1¼ cups freshly squeezed pink grapefruit juice |
|---|---|---|

1. ***Make the granita.*** In a small saucepan over medium-high heat, combine the water and sugar and bring to a boil. Cook, stirring frequently, until the sugar dissolves. Remove the pan from the heat and let cool for several minutes. Place the grapefruit juice in a medium bowl. Add the cooled syrup to the juice and stir to mix well.

2. ***Freeze.*** Transfer the granita to the stainless steel bowl and cover with plastic wrap. Freeze for at least 6 hours, stirring and breaking up the ice crystals with a fork every hour or so.

3. ***Serve.*** To serve, use a fork to scrape the frozen mixture into two cocktail glasses. Serve immediately.

## Tip

Add a splash of vodka to turn this light dessert into an after-dinner cocktail.

# Strawberry Champagne Granita

**EQUIPMENT/TOOLS: BLENDER OR FOOD PROCESSOR, FINE-MESH SIEVE, MINI LOAF PAN, PLASTIC WRAP, TWO CHAMPAGNE COUPES OR COCKTAIL GLASSES**

**Makes 2 servings** • **Prep time: 5 minutes, plus 6 hours to freeze** •
**No-Bake, Lightly Sweet**

Strawberries and champagne combine to make a fruity and light dessert that is perfect for a celebration. I love to serve this in wide champagne glasses (coupes) for a fun and festive presentation.

1 cup diced fresh strawberries

2½ tablespoons granulated sugar

1 teaspoon freshly squeezed lemon juice

1¼ cups champagne or other sparkling wine

1. ***Make the strawberry-champagne mixture.*** In a blender or food processor, combine the strawberries, sugar, and lemon juice and blend until smooth. Strain through a fine-meshed sieve into a metal loaf pan. Whisk in the champagne.

2. ***Freeze.*** Cover the pan with plastic wrap. Freeze for at least 6 hours, stirring and breaking up the granita with a fork every hour or so.

3. ***Serve.*** To serve, use a fork to scrape the frozen granita into cocktail glasses. Serve immediately.

## *Tip*

This dessert is every bit as good made with raspberries, blackberries, or even peaches.

# Vietnamese Iced Coffee Float

**Makes 2 floats • Prep time: 5 minutes, plus 6 hours to freeze • No-Bake**

Vietnamese coffee is very dark, thick, and strong. The generous splash of sweetened condensed milk turns it into a sweet treat. This dessert replicates those flavors by floating a scoop of sweetened condensed milk ice cream in a cold glass of strong brewed coffee.

½ cup cold heavy
  (whipping) cream
⅓ cup cold sweetened
  condensed milk

1½ cups cold brewed
  coffee (strong)
Cinnamon, for
  garnish (optional)

1. ***Make the ice cream.*** In a medium bowl, use an electric mixer on high to whip the cream until soft peaks form. Add the sweetened condensed milk and whisk the mixture until it forms stiff peaks. Transfer the mixture to a mini loaf pan and cover with plastic wrap. Freeze for at least 6 hours, stirring and breaking up the ice cream with a fork every hour or so.

2. ***Assemble the floats.*** Divide the coffee between two short, wide glasses. Add a large scoop of the ice cream to each glass. Garnish each with a sprinkle of cinnamon (if using). Serve immediately.

## Tip

If you're a regular coffee drinker, just make extra and stash it in the fridge so you can make this treat later on.

# Crispy (Not) Fried Ice Cream

EQUIPMENT/TOOLS: PARCHMENT PAPER, ICE CREAM SCOOP, FOOD PROCESSOR, SKILLET

**Makes 2 servings • Prep time: 5 minutes, plus 30 minutes to freeze •
Cook time: 5 minutes • No-Bake**

Deep-fried ice cream is an amazing juxtaposition of cold, creamy ice cream encased in a crunchy, flash-fried shell. This dessert provides that same creamy and crunchy contrast without the need for a deep fryer. Cornflake cereal tossed with butter, sugar, and cinnamon makes a crunchy outer coating for creamy vanilla ice cream. If you want even more crunch, add finely chopped nuts to the coating.

4 small scoops (about 3 inches) Easy No-Churn Vanilla Ice Cream (page 166) or store-bought ice cream

1 cup cornflake cereal

¼ cup unsalted butter

½ teaspoon cinnamon

1½ tablespoons granulated sugar

Chocolate or caramel sauce and/or whipped cream, for serving (optional)

1. ***Freeze the ice cream balls.*** Line a plate with parchment paper. Scoop the balls of ice cream using a small ice cream scoop or a large cookie scoop. Place the ice cream balls on the prepared plate and freeze for 30 minutes.

2. ***Make the coating.*** In a food processor, pulse the cornflakes several times until they become fine crumbs. In a medium skillet over medium heat, melt the butter. Add the cornflake crumbs and cinnamon and cook, stirring, until the mixture turns golden brown, about 5 minutes. Remove the pan from the heat and immediately stir in the sugar. Transfer to a shallow bowl and set aside to cool to room temperature.

3. ***Coat the ice cream balls.*** Roll the frozen ice cream balls in the cooled cornflakes, pressing the coating into the ice cream so that it fully covers the balls. Serve immediately, garnished with sauce or whipped cream (if using).

## *Equipment Hack*

Use a resealable plastic bag and rolling pin to make the cornflake crumbs instead of a food processor.

# Piña Colada Ice Pops

**Makes 2 ice pops • Prep time: 5 minutes, plus 6 hours to freeze •
No-Bake, Lightly Sweet**

If you like piña coladas, and getting caught in the rain . . . Oops, sorry, I thought I was writing a personal ad for a second there. These ice pops taste just like everyone's favorite tropical cocktail, but in the form of a frozen dessert. If you've been looking for a special someone to escape with, this dessert will get their attention.

¼ cup pineapple juice

2 tablespoons
  granulated sugar

⅓ cup full-fat coconut milk

1 teaspoon freshly squeezed
  lime juice

1 tablespoon white
  rum (optional)

1. ***Combine the ingredients.*** In a small saucepan over medium heat, combine the pineapple juice and sugar and heat, stirring frequently, until the sugar dissolves. Remove the pan from the heat and let cool. Stir in the coconut milk, lime juice, and rum (if using).

2. ***Freeze and serve.*** Pour the mixture into your freezing vessel. Insert the sticks and freeze for at least 6 hours. Serve frozen.

## Equipment Hack

Use small paper cups and wooden ice pop sticks instead.

## Tip

If you want the rum flavor but don't want to add rum, use ¼ teaspoon of rum extract instead. You can usually find rum extract in the supermarket alongside vanilla and other extracts.

# Very Berry Frozen Yogurt Ice Pops

**EQUIPMENT/TOOLS: TWO ICE POP MOLDS**

**Makes 2 ice pops** • **Prep time: 5 minutes, plus 6 hours to freeze** •
**No-Bake, Lightly Sweet**

Made with plain yogurt, fresh berries, and a drizzle of honey, these ice pops are as healthy as they are delicious. They're also pretty to look at. That they are so easy to put together makes them a no-brainer. They're a great light refresher on a warm summer day.

¼ cup full-fat plain yogurt

½ cup fresh berries (such as strawberries, blueberries,

raspberries, blackberries, or a combination)

1 to 3 teaspoons honey

1. ***Mix the yogurt and fruit.*** In a small bowl, add the yogurt and berries and stir to combine. Add a teaspoon of honey and stir to incorporate. Taste and add additional honey, if desired.

2. ***Freeze.*** Pour the mixture into your freezing vessels. Insert the sticks and freeze for at least 6 hours. Serve frozen.

## Equipment Hack

Use small paper cups and wooden ice pop sticks instead.

## Tip

You can make these dairy-free by using soy or coconut yogurt instead of cow's milk yogurt.

# *Frozen Strawberry Cheesecake Pops*

EQUIPMENT/TOOLS: BLENDER OR FOOD PROCESSOR, TWO ICE POP MOLDS

**Makes 2 cheesecake pops · Prep time: 5 minutes, plus 6 hours to freeze · No-Bake**

Strawberry cheesecake is a dreamy dessert, to be sure, but turn it into frozen ice pops and you've got something really special. Just a handful of ingredients and 5 minutes of hands-on time will produce a rich, creamy, but also refreshingly fruity frozen dessert I hope you'll love as much as I do.

½ cup diced strawberries

1½ ounces cream cheese, at room temperature

¼ cup sweetened condensed milk

1½ tablespoons plain yogurt

¼ teaspoon vanilla extract

1. ***Make the cheesecake mixture.*** In a blender or food processor, purée the strawberries until smooth. Add the cream cheese, sweetened condensed milk, yogurt, and vanilla and process just until the mixture is well combined and smooth.

2. ***Freeze.*** Pour the mixture into your freezing vessels. Insert the sticks and freeze for at least 6 hours. Serve frozen.

## *Equipment Hack*

Use small paper cups and wooden ice pop sticks instead.

## *Tip*

You can make pretty layered pops by keeping the strawberry purée separate from the cream cheese and milk mixture and then adding the two in alternating layers to the ice pop molds.

# Frozen Fudge Pops

**Makes 2 fudge pops** • **Prep time: 5 minutes, plus 6 hours to freeze** •
**No-Bake, Lightly Sweet**

A combination of semisweet chocolate and unsweetened cocoa powder give these frozen fudge pops a deep, rich, chocolatey flavor. They're just the thing when you want a cold, refreshing, no-fuss dessert.

⅔ cup whole milk

1 tablespoon unsweetened
  cocoa powder

2 tablespoons semisweet
  chocolate chips, melted

¼ teaspoon vanilla extract

1. **Make the ice pop mixture.** In a medium microwave-safe bowl, heat the milk until very hot, about 2 minutes. Whisk in the cocoa powder until it dissolves completely. Add the chocolate chips and stir until they melt completely and the mixture is smooth. Stir in the vanilla.

2. **Freeze and serve.** Pour the mixture into your freezing vessels. Insert the sticks and freeze for at least 6 hours. Serve frozen.

## Equipment Hack

Use small paper cups and wooden ice pop sticks instead.

## Tip

You can use any type of milk in these that you like—whether that is low-fat cow's milk or plant-based milks like almond, soy, or coconut.

# Classic Ice Cream Sandwiches

EQUIPMENT/TOOLS: PLASTIC WRAP, BAKING SHEET,
PARCHMENT PAPER, ROLLING PIN, WIRE RACK

**Makes 2 sandwiches • Prep time: 20 minutes, plus 4½ hours to freeze •
Cook time: 8 to 10 minutes**

A classic ice cream sandwich is made by sandwiching vanilla ice cream between two chocolate cookies. It's one of the most perfect desserts ever made and needs no further adornment. But don't let me stop you from garnishing the edges with mini chocolate chips or rainbow sprinkles. Sky's the limit.

**FOR THE COOKIES**

¼ cup plus 2 tablespoons
  all-purpose flour, plus
  additional for dusting

1 tablespoon plus 1 teaspoon
  unsweetened cocoa powder

⅛ teaspoon baking soda

Pinch kosher salt

2 tablespoons unsalted butter,
  at room temperature

2½ tablespoons
  granulated sugar

1 teaspoon light corn syrup

1 large egg yolk

¼ teaspoon vanilla extract

2 large scoops Easy No-Churn
  Vanilla Ice Cream (page 166)
  or store-bought ice cream

1. **Make the cookie dough.** In a small bowl, whisk together the flour, cocoa powder, baking soda, and salt. In a medium bowl, cream together the butter, sugar, and corn syrup until fluffy and pale. Beat in the egg yolk and vanilla. Add the dry ingredients to the butter mixture and beat to combine. Form the dough into a ball, wrap in plastic wrap, and chill for 30 minutes.

2. **Preheat the oven and prepare the baking sheet.** Preheat the oven to 350°F. Line the baking sheet with parchment paper.

3. **Bake the cookies.** Place the chilled dough on a lightly floured surface. Roll out the dough to about ⅛-inch thick. Place on the prepared baking sheet and bake for 8 to 10 minutes, until the edges are set. Let cool on the baking sheet on a wire rack.

4. ***Assemble the ice cream sandwiches.*** Line a plate with parchment paper. Cut the cookie into four rectangles, about 3×2 inches each. Scoop the ice cream into a bowl and stir for a couple of minutes, just until it softens. Turn two of the cookie rectangles bottom-side up and place a scoop of ice cream on each, flattening the top slightly. Top the ice cream with the remaining cookie rectangles and gently press down. Place the sandwiches on the prepared plate and freeze for at least 4 hours, until set. Serve frozen.

You can make ice cream sandwiches using just about any cookie and ice cream combo that strikes your fancy. I think Spicy Ginger Cookies (page 28) or store-bought ginger-snaps make great ice cream sandwich cookies, myself.

# Ginger-Lemon Ice Cream Cake

**Makes 2 servings • Prep time: 5 minutes, plus 6 hours to freeze •**
**Mini Equipment, No-Bake, Lightly Sweet**

Ice cream cake is the obvious way to celebrate someone born at the height of summer. I'm one of those lucky people with an August birthday, so this cake tops my birthday wish list. The fresh brightness of the lemon ice cream along with the tangy spiciness of the ginger cookies makes for a truly happy birthday. I suggest using Meyer lemons, which are sweeter and have a floral component that complements the gingersnaps well.

**FOR THE CRUST**

12 gingersnaps, crushed into crumbs, divided

2 tablespoons unsalted butter, melted

**FOR THE ICE CREAM**

¼ cup sweetened condensed milk

1 teaspoon grated lemon zest

1 tablespoon freshly squeezed lemon juice

½ cup cold heavy (whipping) cream

1. ***Make the crust.*** In a small bowl, stir together all but 2 tablespoons of the cookie crumbs and the butter. Press the mixture into the bottom and up the sides of your chosen vessel(s).

2. ***Make the ice cream.*** In a small bowl, stir together the sweetened condensed milk, lemon zest, and lemon juice. In a medium bowl, use an electric mixer on high to whip the cream until soft peaks form. Using a rubber spatula, fold a dollop of the whipped cream into the condensed milk mixture. Add the condensed milk mixture to the whipped cream and continue to whip until stiff peaks form.

3. ***Assemble and freeze.*** Transfer the mixture into the prepared crust and smooth out the top. Sprinkle the reserved 2 tablespoons of cookie crumbs over the top. Cover with plastic wrap and freeze for at least 6 hours.

4. ***Serve.*** Let the cake stand at room temperature for about 10 minutes before serving. Cut into wedges and serve.

## Equipment Hack

Use two 8-ounce ramekins or widemouthed canning jars instead.

# Cookies and Cream
# Ice Cream Cake

EQUIPMENT/TOOLS: MINI ROUND CAKE PAN, ELECTRIC MIXER

**Makes 2 servings • Prep time: 15 minutes, plus 7 hours to freeze • Mini Equipment, No-Bake**

Like me, my son has an August birthday, and this is his cake of choice. Chocolate wafer cookies make the flavorful crust. A sweet, creamy vanilla ice cream studded with bits of chocolate wafer cookies fills out the cake. The chocolate ganache topping is what really puts a smile on his face.

**FOR THE CRUST**

18 chocolate wafers, crushed into crumbs

2 tablespoons unsalted butter, melted

**FOR THE ICE CREAM**

¼ cup sweetened condensed milk

¼ teaspoon vanilla extract

½ cup cold heavy (whipping) cream

8 chocolate wafers, broken into small pieces

**FOR CHOCOLATE TOPPING**

¼ cup heavy (whipping) cream

4 ounces semisweet chocolate, finely chopped

¼ teaspoon vanilla extract

1. ***Make the crust.*** In a small bowl, stir together all but 2 tablespoons of the cookie crumbs and the butter. Press the mixture into the bottom and up the sides of your chosen vessel(s).

2. ***Make the ice cream.*** In a small bowl, stir together the sweetened condensed milk and vanilla. In a medium bowl, use an electric mixer on high to whip the cream until soft peaks form. Using a rubber spatula, fold a dollop of the whipped cream into the condensed milk mixture. Add the condensed milk mixture to the whipped cream and continue to whip until stiff peaks form. Add the broken cookie pieces and stir to mix.

3. ***Assemble and freeze.*** Spread the ice cream mixture into the crust and cover with plastic wrap. Freeze for at least 6 hours.

➤

4. ***Make the topping.*** In a microwave-safe bowl, combine the cream and chocolate. Microwave in 30-second intervals, stirring in between, until the chocolate is completely melted and the mixture is smooth. Stir in the vanilla. While the chocolate sauce is still a bit warm, pour it over the ice cream and spread it into an even layer. Freeze for 1 hour more.

5. ***Serve.*** Let the cake stand at room temperature for 10 minutes before serving. Cut into wedges and serve.

## Equipment Hack

Use two 8-ounce ramekins or widemouthed canning jars instead.

# *Frozen Raspberry Hot Chocolate*

EQUIPMENT/TOOLS: SMALL SAUCEPAN, DOUBLE BOILER OR BOWL SET OVER SIMMERING WATER, BLENDER, 2 WATER GOBLETS OR OTHER GLASSES

**Makes 2 servings • Prep time: 10 minutes • Cook time: 5 minutes • Quick, No-Bake**

Frozen hot chocolate sounds just plain silly, but it turns out that it is utterly delicious. A chocolatey milk mixture is infused with puréed raspberries and then blended with ice into a veritable chocolate smoothie. It's topped with whipped cream and a drizzle of raspberry sauce. Yum.

**FOR THE RASPBERRY SAUCE**

¼ cup raspberry jam

1½ teaspoons water

**FOR THE FROZEN HOT CHOCOLATE**

3 ounces semisweet chocolate, finely chopped

1 tablespoon unsweetened cocoa powder

1½ tablespoons granulated sugar

1½ cups milk, divided

½ cup fresh raspberries

3 cups ice

**FOR SERVING**

Whipped cream

Chocolate shavings

1. *Make the raspberry sauce.* In a small saucepan over medium heat, combine the raspberry jam and water and heat, stirring frequently, until the jam is melted and the mixture is smooth.

2. *Make the frozen hot chocolate.* In a double boiler or in a heat-proof bowl set over a pot of simmering water, melt the chocolate, stirring frequently. Add the cocoa powder and sugar and stir until smooth and well combined. Remove from the heat and stir in ½ cup of the milk. Set the mixture aside to cool to room temperature. Meanwhile, place the remaining cup of milk in a blender with the raspberries. Add the cooled chocolate mixture and the ice and blend on high until the mixture is smooth and thick.

3. *Serve.* Pour the mixture into your serving vessels. Top each with a dollop of whipped cream. Drizzle the raspberry sauce over the whipped cream and then finish with a sprinkle of chocolate shavings. Serve immediately.

## *Tip*

**Make this a frozen mint hot chocolate by replacing the raspberry sauce with ¼ teaspoon of peppermint extract. Add crushed candy canes as a garnish.**

# Measurement Conversions

| | U.S. STANDARD | U.S. STANDARD (OUNCES) | METRIC (APPROXIMATE) |
|---|---|---|---|
| **VOLUME EQUIVALENTS (LIQUID)** | 2 tablespoons | 1 fl. oz. | 30 mL |
| | ¼ cup | 2 fl. oz. | 60 mL |
| | ½ cup | 4 fl. oz. | 120 mL |
| | 1 cup | 8 fl. oz. | 240 mL |
| | 1½ cups | 12 fl. oz. | 355 mL |
| | 2 cups or 1 pint | 16 fl. oz. | 475 mL |
| | 4 cups or 1 quart | 32 fl. oz. | 1 L |
| | 1 gallon | 128 fl. oz. | 4 L |
| **VOLUME EQUIVALENTS (DRY)** | ⅛ teaspoon | ———— | 0.5 mL |
| | ¼ teaspoon | ———— | 1 mL |
| | ½ teaspoon | ———— | 2 mL |
| | ¾ teaspoon | ———— | 4 mL |
| | 1 teaspoon | ———— | 5 mL |
| | 1 tablespoon | ———— | 15 mL |
| | ¼ cup | ———— | 59 mL |
| | ⅓ cup | ———— | 79 mL |
| | ½ cup | ———— | 118 mL |
| | ⅔ cup | ———— | 156 mL |
| | ¾ cup | ———— | 177 mL |
| | 1 cup | ———— | 235 mL |
| | 2 cups or 1 pint | ———— | 475 mL |
| | 3 cups | ———— | 700 mL |
| | 4 cups or 1 quart | ———— | 1 L |
| | ½ gallon | ———— | 2 L |
| | 1 gallon | ———— | 4 L |
| **WEIGHT EQUIVALENTS** | ½ ounce | ———— | 15 g |
| | 1 ounce | ———— | 30 g |
| | 2 ounces | ———— | 60 g |
| | 4 ounces | ———— | 115 g |
| | 8 ounces | ———— | 225 g |
| | 12 ounces | ———— | 340 g |
| | 16 ounces or 1 pound | ———— | 455 g |

# *Fruity, Chocolatey, or Creamy?*

**Chocolatey**

Caramel Swirl Brownies, 42
Chocolate-Covered Strawberry
  Cheesecake Bites, 131
Chocolate-Hazelnut Filled Scones,
  122–123
Chocolate-Hazelnut Mug
  Cakes, 79
Chocolate Mousse Pie, 99–100
Chocolate-Orange Sorbet, 171
Chocolate Soufflés, 147–148
Classic Chocolate Truffles with
  Hazelnuts, 133
Classic Double Chocolate
  Brownies, 39
Classic Ice Cream Sandwiches,
  180–181
Cocoa Cutout Cookies, 36
Coconut Almond Chocolate Chunk
  Cookies, 31
Coffee and Cream Brownies, 40–41
Cookies and Cream Ice Cream
  Cake, 183–184
Dark Chocolate Almond Butter
  Cups, 134
Dark Chocolate Cherry Bark, 140
Dark Chocolate Cherry Tartlet, 114
Dark Chocolate Pudding, 157
Double Chocolate Cookies, 29
Frozen Fudge Pops, 179
Frozen Raspberry Hot
  Chocolate, 185
Hot Fudge Brownie Sundaes with
  Spiced Candied Pecans, 169–170
Lemon White Chocolate
  Truffles, 132
Marshmallow-Filled Chocolate
  Cupcakes, 58–59
Mocha Meringue Kisses, 37
Molten Lava Cakes, 78
No-Bake Chocolate Peanut Butter
  Bars, 51
Peppermint Chocolate Bark, 139
Rocky Road Fudge, 138
S'mores Cakes, 82–83
Stay-at-Home S'mores, 135–136
Strawberry and Dark Chocolate
  Hand Pies, 103–104

Very Best Chocolate Chip Cookies,
  The, 24–25
White Chocolate and Toasted
  Almond Fudge. *See also* White
  chocolate
White Chocolate Butter Cookies, 35

**Creamy**

Banana and Butterscotch Pudding
  Parfaits, 154
Banana Cream Mini Pies, 92–93
Berries in Coconut Cream, 144
Caramel Apple Yogurt Parfaits, 155
Chocolate Mousse Pie, 99–100
Classic Ice Cream Sandwiches,
  180–181
Coconut Rice Pudding with Fresh
  Mangos, 151
Cookies and Cream Ice Cream
  Cake, 183–184
Crispy (Not) Fried Ice Cream, 175
Dark Chocolate Pudding, 157
Easy No-Churn Vanilla Ice
  Cream, 166
Espresso Custard, 152
Ginger-Lemon Ice Cream
  Cake, 182
Grilled Peach Sundaes with
  Bourbon Caramel Sauce,
  167–168
Hot Fudge Brownie Sundaes with
  Spiced Candied Pecans, 169–170
Lemon Curd Tarts, 109
Lemon Meringue Mini Pies,
  94–95
Lemon Pudding Cakes, 85
Maple Pecan Tapioca Pudding, 156
Mini Pumpkin Cheesecakes, 68
Mixed Berry and Pastry Cream
  Tartlet, 112–113
No-Bake Key Lime Pie Cups, 105
No-Bake Tiramisu Cheesecakes,
  69–70
Orange Panna Cotta, 153
Pumpkin Flan, 159–160
Pumpkin Mini Pies, 96
Salted Caramel Pots de Crème, 158
Strawberry Mousse, 145
Whipped Lemon Ricotta Mousse.
  *See also* Ricotta cheese

**Fruity**

Apple Pie Bars, 45–46
Apples and Honey Cupcakes with
  Cinnamon Buttercream, 56–57
Banana and Butterscotch Pudding
  Parfaits, 154
Banana Cream Mini Pies, 92–93
Berries in Coconut Cream, 144
Blackberry Cobbler, 117
Blackberry Vanilla Bread
  Pudding, 149
Blueberry Cheesecake Bars, 47
Blueberry Yogurt Cake, 73
Bourbon Peach Cobbler, 118
Brown Sugar Cinnamon Stuffed
  Apple Crisp, 115
Chocolate-Covered Strawberry
  Cheesecake Bites, 131
Chocolate-Orange Sorbet, 171
Cinnamon Pear Galettes, 106
Coffee-Poached Pears with
  Caramel Syrup, 162
Dark Chocolate Cherry Bark, 140
Dark Chocolate Cherry Tartlet, 114
Fig, Honey, and Blue Cheese
  Galettes, 107–108
Frozen Raspberry Hot
  Chocolate, 185
Frozen Strawberry Cheesecake
  Pops, 178
Ginger-Lemon Ice Cream
  Cake, 182
Graham Cracker Lime Icebox
  Cake, 84
Grilled Peach Sundaes with
  Bourbon Caramel Sauce,
  167–168
Lattice-Topped Mini Blueberry
  Pies, 88–89
Lemon Bars with Toasted
  Almonds, 43–44
Lemon Curd Tarts, 109
Lemon Meringue Mini Pies,
  94–95
Lemon Pudding Cakes, 85
Lemon Shortbread Cookies, 30
Lemon White Chocolate
  Truffles, 132

**Fruity** *(Continued)*

Mimosa Cupcakes with Champagne-Orange Butter-cream, 66–67

Mini Pineapple Upside-Down Cakes, 74

Mixed Berry and Pastry Cream Tartlet, 112–113

Mixed Berry Summer Pudding, 163

No-Bake Key Lime Pie Cups, 105

Peach Hand Pies, 101–102

Pear and Coconut Crisp, 116

Piña Colada Ice Pops, 176

Pink Grapefruit Granita, 172

Raspberry Jam–Filled Mini Tartlets, 110–111

Sour Cream Apple Mini Pies, 90–91

Strawberry and Dark Chocolate Hand Pies, 103–104

Strawberry Balsamic Sorbet, 170

Strawberry Champagne Granita, 173

Strawberry Clafoutis, 161

Strawberry Mousse, 145

Strawberry Rhubarb Crumble, 119

Strawberry Shortcakes, 129

Very Berry Frozen Yogurt Ice Pops, 177

Whipped Lemon Ricotta Mousse. *See also* Ricotta cheese

Whole-Wheat Oatmeal Cookies with Dried Blueberries, 27

# Just Egg White, Just Egg Yolk, Small Amount of Flour?

**Just egg whites**

Apples and Honey Cupcakes with Cinnamon Buttercream, 56–57
Classic Vanilla Cupcakes with Buttercream, 54–55
Coconut Almond Chocolate Chunk Cookies, 31
Coconut Cupcakes with Coconut Buttercream, 60–61
Marshmallow-Filled Chocolate Cupcakes, 58–59
Mimosa Cupcakes with Champagne-Orange Buttercream, 66–67
Mini Carrot Cakes, 75–76
Mini Pineapple Upside-Down Cakes, 74
Mocha Meringue Kisses, 37
Peach Hand Pies, 101–102
Salted Caramel Cupcakes, 62–63
Spiced Chai Cupcakes, 64–65
Spicy Ginger Cookies, 28

**Just egg yolks**

Banana and Butterscotch Pudding Parfaits, 154
Banana Cream Mini Pies, 92–93
Blueberry Cheesecake Bars, 47
Butterscotch Blondies, 38
Caramel Swirl Brownies, 42
Chocolate-Hazelnut Filled Scones, 122–123
Classic Double Chocolate Brownies, 39
Classic Ice Cream Sandwiches, 180–181

Coffee and Cream Brownies, 40–41
Dark Chocolate Cherry Tartlet, 114
Double Chocolate Cookies, 29
Espresso Custard, 152
Flourless Peanut Butter Cookies, 26
Graham Cracker Lime Icebox Cake, 84
Mixed Berry and Pastry Cream Tartlet, 112–113
Molten Lava Cakes, 78
Pumpkin Flan, 159–160
Red Velvet Layer Bars, 50
Salted Caramel Pots de Crème, 158
Very Best Chocolate Chip Cookies, The, 24–25
Whole-Wheat Oatmeal Cookies with Dried Blueberries, 27

**½ cup or less of flour**

Apples and Honey Cupcakes with Cinnamon Buttercream, 56–57
Blackberry Cobbler, 117
Bourbon Peach Cobbler, 118
Brown Sugar Cinnamon Stuffed Apple Crisp, 115
Butterscotch Blondies, 38
Caramel Swirl Brownies, 42
Chocolate-Hazelnut Filled Scones, 122–123
Chocolate-Hazelnut Mug Cakes, 79
Classic Double Chocolate Brownies, 39
Classic Vanilla Cupcakes with Buttercream, 54–55

Cocoa Cutout Cookies, 36
Coconut Cupcakes with Coconut Buttercream, 60–61
Coffee and Cream Brownies, 40–41
Coffee Crumb Cake. *See also* Espresso powder
Double Chocolate Cookies, 29
Lemon Pudding Cakes, 85
Lemon Shortbread Cookies, 30
Maple-Glazed Donuts, 126
Marshmallow-Filled Chocolate Cupcakes, 58–59
Mexican Wedding Cookies, 33–34
Mimosa Cupcakes with Champagne-Orange Buttercream, 66–67
Mini Pineapple Upside-Down Cakes, 74
Molten Lava Cakes, 78
Peanut Butter Banana Cakes, 81
Pear and Coconut Crisp, 116
Red Velvet Layer Bars, 50
Red Velvet Mug Cakes, 80
Salted Caramel Cupcakes, 62–63
S'mores Cakes, 82–83
Spiced Chai Cupcakes, 64–65
Strawberry Clafoutis, 161
Strawberry Rhubarb Crumble, 119
Toffee Pecan Sandies, 32
Very Best Chocolate Chip Cookies, The, 24–25
White Chocolate Butter Cookies, 35
Whole-Wheat Oatmeal Cookies with Dried Blueberries, 27

# General Index

## A

Almond butter
  Dark Chocolate Almond Butter
    Cups, 134
Almonds
  Coconut Almond Chocolate Chunk
    Cookies, 31
  Dark Chocolate Cherry Bark, 140
  Lemon Bars with Toasted
    Almonds, 43–44
  Mexican Wedding Cookies, 33–34
  White Chocolate and Toasted
    Almond Fudge, 137
Apple Pie Bars, 45–46
Apples
  Apple Pie Bars, 45–46
  Apples and Honey Cupcakes with
    Cinnamon Buttercream, 56–57
  Brown Sugar Cinnamon Stuffed
    Apple Crisp, 115
  Caramel Apple Yogurt Parfaits, 155
  Sour Cream Apple Mini Pies,
    90–91

## B

Baking sheets, 5
Bananas
  Banana and Butterscotch Pudding
    Parfaits, 154
  Banana Cream Mini Pies, 92–93
  Peanut Butter Banana Cakes, 81
Bars. See also Brownies
  Apple Pie Bars, 45–46
  Blueberry Cheesecake Bars, 47
  Caramel Crumb Bars, 48–49
  Lemon Bars with Toasted
    Almonds, 43–44
  No-Bake Chocolate Peanut Butter
    Bars, 51
  Red Velvet Layer Bars, 50
  storing, 9
Berries
  Berries in Coconut Cream, 144
  Blackberry Cobbler, 117
  Blackberry Vanilla Bread
    Pudding, 149
  Blueberry Cheesecake Bars, 47
  Blueberry Yogurt Cake, 73
  Chocolate-Covered Strawberry
    Cheesecake Bites, 131
  Frozen Raspberry Hot
    Chocolate, 185

Frozen Strawberry Cheesecake
  Pops, 178
Lattice-Topped Mini Blueberry
  Pies, 88–89
Mixed Berry and Pastry Cream
  Tartlet, 112–113
Mixed Berry Summer
  Pudding, 163
Raspberry Jam–Filled Mini
  Tartlets, 110–111
Strawberry and Dark Chocolate
  Hand Pies, 103–104
Strawberry Balsamic Sorbet, 170
Strawberry Champagne
  Granita, 173
Strawberry Clafoutis, 161
Strawberry Mousse, 145
Strawberry Rhubarb
  Crumble, 119
Strawberry Shortcakes, 129
Very Berry Frozen Yogurt Ice
  Pops, 177
Whole-Wheat Oatmeal Cookies
  with Dried Blueberries, 27
Blackberry Cobbler, 117
Blackberry Vanilla Bread
  Pudding, 149
Blind baking, 18
Blueberry Cheesecake Bars, 47
Blueberry Yogurt Cake, 73
Bourbon Peach Cobbler, 118
Bourbon Pecan Pie, 97–98
Bread puddings
  Blackberry Vanilla Bread
    Pudding, 149
  Butterscotch Bread
    Pudding, 150
  Mixed Berry Summer
    Pudding, 163
Brownies
  Butterscotch Blondies, 38
  Caramel Swirl Brownies, 42
  Classic Double Chocolate
    Brownies, 39
  Coffee and Cream Brownies,
    40–41
  storing, 9
Brown sugar, storing, 6–7
Brown Sugar Cinnamon Stuffed
  Apple Crisp, 115
Butterscotch Blondies, 38
Butterscotch Bread Pudding, 150

## C

Cake pans, 4
Cakes. See also Cheesecakes;
    Cupcakes
  Blueberry Yogurt Cake, 73
  Chocolate-Hazelnut Mug
    Cakes, 79
  Coffee Crumb Cake, 71–72
  Cookies and Cream Ice Cream
    Cake, 183–184
  frosting, 18–19
  Ginger-Lemon Ice Cream
    Cake, 182
  Graham Cracker Lime Icebox
    Cake, 84
  Lemon Pudding Cakes, 85
  Mini Carrot Cakes, 75–76
  Mini Confetti Cakes, 77
  Mini Pineapple Upside-Down
    Cakes, 74
  Molten Lava Cakes, 78
  Peanut Butter Banana Cakes, 81
  Red Velvet Mug Cakes, 80
  S'mores Cakes, 82–83
  storing, 9
Canning jar lids and rings, 5
Caramel Apple Yogurt
  Parfaits, 155
Caramel Crumb Bars, 48–49
Caramel Swirl Brownies, 42
Carrots
  Mini Carrot Cakes, 75–76
Champagne
  Mimosa Cupcakes with
    Champagne-Orange Butter-
    cream, 66–67
  Strawberry Champagne
    Granita, 173
Cheese. See also Cream cheese;
    Mascarpone cheese; Ricotta
    cheese
  Fig, Honey, and Blue Cheese
    Galettes, 107–108
Cheesecakes
  Blueberry Cheesecake Bars, 47
  Chocolate-Covered Strawberry
    Cheesecake Bites, 131
  Frozen Strawberry Cheesecake
    Pops, 178
  Mini Pumpkin Cheesecakes, 68
  No-Bake Tiramisu Cheesecakes,
    69–70

Cherries
  Dark Chocolate Cherry Bark, 140
  Dark Chocolate Cherry Tartlet, 114
Chocolate. *See also* White chocolate
  Caramel Swirl Brownies, 42
  Chocolate-Covered Strawberry
    Cheesecake Bites, 131
  Chocolate-Hazelnut Mug
    Cakes, 79
  Chocolate Mousse Pie, 99–100
  Chocolate-Orange Sorbet, 171
  Chocolate Soufflés, 147–148
  Classic Chocolate Truffles with
    Hazelnuts, 133
  Classic Double Chocolate
    Brownies, 39
  Classic Ice Cream Sandwiches,
    180–181
  Cocoa Cutout Cookies, 36
  Coconut Almond Chocolate Chunk
    Cookies, 31
  Coffee and Cream Brownies, 40–41
  Cookies and Cream Ice Cream
    Cake, 183–184
  Dark Chocolate Almond Butter
    Cups, 134
  Dark Chocolate Cherry Bark, 140
  Dark Chocolate Cherry Tartlet, 114
  Dark Chocolate Pudding, 157
  Double Chocolate Cookies, 29
  Frozen Fudge Pops, 179
  Frozen Raspberry Hot
    Chocolate, 185
  Hot Fudge Brownie Sundaes with
    Spiced Candied Pecans, 169–170
  Marshmallow-Filled Chocolate
    Cupcakes, 58–59
  melting, 14
  Mocha Meringue Kisses, 37
  Molten Lava Cakes, 78
  No-Bake Chocolate Peanut Butter
    Bars, 51
  Peppermint Chocolate Bark, 139
  Red Velvet Layer Bars, 50
  Red Velvet Mug Cakes, 80
  Rocky Road Fudge, 138
  S'mores Cakes, 82–83
  Stay-at-Home S'mores, 135–136
  Strawberry and Dark Chocolate
    Hand Pies, 103–104
  Very Best Chocolate Chip Cookies,
    The, 24–25
Chocolate-Hazelnut Filled Scones,
  122–123
Chocolate-Hazelnut Mug Cakes, 79
Chocolate-Orange Sorbet, 171
Cinnamon Pear Galettes, 106

Cinnamon Sugar Monkey Bread,
  127–128
Classic Chocolate Truffles with
  Hazelnuts, 133
Classic Double Chocolate
  Brownies, 39
Classic Ice Cream Sandwiches,
  180–181
Classic Vanilla Cupcakes with
  Buttercream, 54–55
Cocoa Cutout Cookies, 36
Coconut
  Coconut Almond Chocolate Chunk
    Cookies, 31
  Coconut Cupcakes with Coconut
    Buttercream, 60–61
  Pear and Coconut Crisp, 116
  Red Velvet Layer Bars, 50
Coconut milk
  Berries in Coconut Cream, 144
  Coconut Cupcakes with Coconut
    Buttercream, 60–61
  Coconut Rice Pudding with Fresh
    Mangos, 151
  Piña Colada Ice Pops, 176
Coffee. *See also* Espresso powder
  Coffee Crumb Cake, 71–72
  Coffee-Poached Pears with
    Caramel Syrup, 162
  Vietnamese Iced Coffee Float, 174
Coffee and Cinnamon Rolls, 124–125
Coffee and Cream Brownies, 40–41
Confections
  Chocolate-Covered Strawberry
    Cheesecake Bites, 131
  Classic Chocolate Truffles with
    Hazelnuts, 133
  Dark Chocolate Almond Butter
    Cups, 134
  Dark Chocolate Cherry Bark, 140
  Lemon White Chocolate
    Truffles, 132
  Peppermint Chocolate Bark, 139
  Rocky Road Fudge, 138
  Stay-at-Home S'mores, 135–136
  White Chocolate and Toasted
    Almond Fudge, 137
Cookies. *See also* Bars
  Cocoa Cutout Cookies, 36
  Coconut Almond Chocolate Chunk
    Cookies, 31
  decorating, 19
  Double Chocolate Cookies, 29
  Flourless Peanut Butter
    Cookies, 26
  Lemon Shortbread Cookies, 30
  Mexican Wedding Cookies, 33–34

  Mocha Meringue Kisses, 37
  Spicy Ginger Cookies, 28
  storing, 9
  Toffee Pecan Sandies, 32
  Very Best Chocolate Chip Cookies,
    The, 24–25
  White Chocolate Butter Cookies, 35
  Whole-Wheat Oatmeal Cookies
    with Dried Blueberries, 27
Cookies and Cream Ice Cream Cake,
  183–184
Cream cheese
  Blueberry Cheesecake Bars, 47
  Chocolate-Covered Strawberry
    Cheesecake Bites, 131
  Coffee and Cream Brownies, 40–41
  Frozen Strawberry Cheesecake
    Pops, 178
  Mini Carrot Cakes, 75–76
  Mini Pumpkin Cheesecakes, 68
  No-Bake Key Lime Pie Cups, 105
  No-Bake Tiramisu Cheesecakes,
    69–70
Creaming, 15
Crisps, cobblers, and crumbles
  Blackberry Cobbler, 117
  Bourbon Peach Cobbler, 118
  Brown Sugar Cinnamon Stuffed
    Apple Crisp, 115
  Pear and Coconut Crisp, 116
  Strawberry Rhubarb Crumble, 119
Crispy (Not) Fried Ice Cream, 175
Cupcakes
  Apples and Honey Cupcakes with
    Cinnamon Buttercream, 56–57
  Classic Vanilla Cupcakes with
    Buttercream, 54–55
  Coconut Cupcakes with Coconut
    Buttercream, 60–61
  frosting, 18–19
  Marshmallow-Filled Chocolate
    Cupcakes, 58–59
  Mimosa Cupcakes with
    Champagne-Orange Butter-
    cream, 66–67
  Salted Caramel Cupcakes, 62–63
  Spiced Chai Cupcakes, 64–65
  storing, 9
Custards
  Espresso Custard, 152
  Orange Panna Cotta, 153
  Pumpkin Flan, 159–160
  Salted Caramel Pots de Crème, 158
  Strawberry Clafoutis, 161
Cutting in, 15

**D**

Dairy products, leftover, 8
Dark Chocolate Almond Butter
    Cups, 134
Dark Chocolate Cherry Bark, 140
Dark Chocolate Cherry
    Tartlet, 114
Dark Chocolate Pudding, 157
Decorating, 18–19
Double-boilers, 14
Double Chocolate Cookies, 29
Dough, 17–18

**E**

Easy No-Churn Vanilla
    Ice Cream, 166
Easy Palmiers, 130
Eggs
    leftover, 8–9
    tempering, 17
    whipping whites, 16
Egg whites
    Coconut Cupcakes with Coconut
        Buttercream, 60–61
Equipment, 4–6
Espresso powder
    Coffee and Cinnamon Rolls,
        124–125
    Coffee and Cream Brownies,
        40–41
    Espresso Custard, 152
    Mocha Meringue Kisses, 37
    No-Bake Tiramisu Cheesecakes,
        69–70

**F**

Fig, Honey, and Blue Cheese
    Galettes, 107–108
Flour, leftover, 9
Flourless Peanut Butter Cookies, 26
Folding, 16
Food processors, 5
Frosting
    Buttercream, 54–55
    Caramel Buttercream, 62–63
    Champagne-Orange Buttercream,
        66–67
    Chocolate Ganache, 58–59
    Cinnamon Buttercream, 56–57
    Coconut Buttercream, 60–61
    techniques, 18–19
Frozen Fudge Pops, 179
Frozen Raspberry Hot
    Chocolate, 185
Frozen Strawberry Cheesecake
    Pops, 178
Fruits, 7. *See also specific*

**G**

Galettes
    Cinnamon Pear Galettes, 106
    Fig, Honey, and Blue Cheese
        Galettes, 107–108
Ginger-Lemon Ice Cream Cake, 182
Gingersnap cookies
    Banana and Butterscotch Pudding
        Parfaits, 154
    Ginger-Lemon Ice Cream
        Cake, 182
    Grilled Peach Sundaes with
        Bourbon Caramel Sauce,
        167–168
    Lemon Curd Tarts, 109
    Mini Pumpkin Cheesecakes, 68
    Pumpkin Mini Pies, 96
Gorgonzola cheese
    Fig, Honey, and Blue Cheese
        Galettes, 107–108
Graham crackers
    Banana Cream Mini Pies, 92–93
    Blueberry Cheesecake Bars, 47
    Graham Cracker Lime Icebox
        Cake, 84
    No-Bake Chocolate Peanut Butter
        Bars, 51
    No-Bake Key Lime Pie Cups, 105
    S'mores Cakes, 82–83
    Stay-at-Home S'mores, 135–136
Granitas
    Pink Grapefruit Granita, 172
    Strawberry Champagne
        Granita, 173
Grapefruits
    Pink Grapefruit Granita, 172
Grilled Peach Sundaes with Bourbon
    Caramel Sauce, 167–168

**H**

Hazelnuts
    Classic Chocolate Truffles with
        Hazelnuts, 133
    Coffee-Poached Pears with
        Caramel Syrup, 162
Hot Fudge Brownie Sundaes with
    Spiced Candied Pecans, 169–170

**I**

Ice cream
    Classic Ice Cream Sandwiches,
        180–181
    Cookies and Cream Ice Cream
        Cake, 183–184
    Crispy (Not) Fried Ice Cream, 175
    Easy No-Churn Vanilla Ice
        Cream, 166

Ginger-Lemon Ice Cream
    Cake, 182
Grilled Peach Sundaes with
    Bourbon Caramel Sauce,
    167–168
Hot Fudge Brownie Sundaes with
    Spiced Candied Pecans, 169–170
Ice pops
    Frozen Fudge Pops, 179
    Frozen Strawberry Cheesecake
        Pops, 178
    molds, 4
    Piña Colada Ice Pops, 176
    Very Berry Frozen Yogurt Ice
        Pops, 177

**L**

Lattice-Topped Mini Blueberry Pies,
    88–89
Leftovers
    desserts, 9–10
    ingredients, 8–9
Lemons
    Apple Pie Bars, 45–46
    Blueberry Yogurt Cake, 73
    Cinnamon Pear Galettes, 106
    Coffee-Poached Pears with
        Caramel Syrup, 162
    Ginger-Lemon Ice Cream
        Cake, 182
    Lemon Bars with Toasted
        Almonds, 43–44
    Lemon Curd Tarts, 109
    Lemon Meringue Mini Pies, 94–95
    Lemon Pudding Cakes, 85
    Lemon Shortbread Cookies, 30
    Lemon White Chocolate
        Truffles, 132
    Mini Confetti Cakes, 77
    Pear and Coconut Crisp, 116
    Strawberry and Dark Chocolate
        Hand Pies, 103–104
    Strawberry Champagne
        Granita, 173
    Whipped Lemon Ricotta
        Mousse, 146
Lightly sweet
    Apples and Honey Cupcakes with
        Cinnamon Buttercream, 56–57
    Berries in Coconut Cream, 144
    Blueberry Yogurt Cake, 73
    Brown Sugar Cinnamon Stuffed
        Apple Crisp, 115
    Cocoa Cutout Cookies, 36
    Espresso Custard, 152
    Fig, Honey, and Blue Cheese
        Galettes, 107–108

Frozen Fudge Pops, 179
Ginger-Lemon Ice Cream Cake, 182
Mixed Berry Summer Pudding, 163
Orange Panna Cotta, 153
Pear and Coconut Crisp, 116
Piña Colada Ice Pops, 176
Pink Grapefruit Granita, 172
Strawberry Champagne
    Granita, 173
Strawberry Clafoutis, 161
Very Berry Frozen Yogurt Ice
    Pops, 177
White Chocolate Butter
    Cookies, 35
Whole-Wheat Oatmeal Cookies
    with Dried Blueberries, 27
Limes
    Graham Cracker Lime Icebox
        Cake, 84
    No-Bake Key Lime Pie Cups, 105
    Piña Colada Ice Pops, 176
Liquid ingredients, mixing, 15–16
Loaf pans, 4

## M

Mangos
    Coconut Rice Pudding with Fresh
        Mangos, 151
Maple-Glazed Donuts, 126
Maple Pecan Tapioca Pudding, 156
Maraschino cherries
    Mini Pineapple Upside-Down
        Cakes, 74
Marshmallows
    Marshmallow-Filled Chocolate
        Cupcakes, 58–59
    Rocky Road Fudge, 138
    S'mores Cakes, 82–83
    Stay-at-Home S'mores, 135–136
Mascarpone cheese
    No-Bake Tiramisu Cheesecakes,
        69–70
Measuring cups and spoons, 5
Melting, chocolate, 14
Mexican Wedding Cookies, 33–34
Mimosa Cupcakes with Champagne-
    Orange Buttercream, 66–67
Mini Carrot Cakes, 75–76
Mini Confetti Cakes, 77
Mini equipment, 4
    Apple Pie Bars, 45–46
    Banana Cream Mini Pies, 92–93
    Blackberry Cobbler, 117
    Blackberry Vanilla Bread
        Pudding, 149
    Blueberry Cheesecake Bars, 47
    Bourbon Peach Cobbler, 118

Bourbon Pecan Pie, 97–98
Caramel Crumb Bars, 48–49
Chocolate Mousse Pie, 99–100
Cinnamon Sugar Monkey Bread,
    127–128
Coffee Crumb Cake, 71–72
Cookies and Cream Ice Cream
    Cake, 183–184
Dark Chocolate Cherry Tartlet, 114
Ginger-Lemon Ice Cream
    Cake, 182
Lemon Bars with Toasted
    Almonds, 43–44
Lemon Curd Tarts, 109
Lemon Meringue Mini Pies,
    94–95
Mixed Berry and Pastry Cream
    Tartlet, 112–113
No-Bake Chocolate Peanut Butter
    Bars, 51
Pumpkin Mini Pies, 96
Raspberry Jam–Filled Mini
    Tartlets, 110–111
Red Velvet Layer Bars, 50
Rocky Road Fudge, 138
Strawberry Rhubarb Crumble, 119
White Chocolate and Toasted
    Almond Fudge, 137
Mini Pineapple Upside-Down
    Cakes, 74
Mini Pumpkin Cheesecakes, 68
Mixed Berry and Pastry Cream
    Tartlet, 112–113
Mixed Berry Summer Pudding, 163
Mixers, 5
Mixing bowls, 5
Mocha Meringue Kisses, 37
Molten Lava Cakes, 78
Mousses
    Strawberry Mousse, 145
    Whipped Lemon Ricotta
        Mousse, 146
Muffins, storing, 9
Muffin tins, 4

## N

No-bake
    Banana and Butterscotch Pudding
        Parfaits, 154
    Berries in Coconut Cream, 144
    Caramel Apple Yogurt Parfaits, 155
    Chocolate-Covered Strawberry
        Cheesecake Bites, 131
    Chocolate Mousse Pie, 99–100
    Chocolate-Orange Sorbet, 171
    Classic Chocolate Truffles with
        Hazelnuts, 133

Coconut Rice Pudding with Fresh
    Mangos, 151
Coffee-Poached Pears with
    Caramel Syrup, 162
Cookies and Cream Ice Cream
    Cake, 183–184
Crispy (Not) Fried Ice Cream, 175
Dark Chocolate Almond Butter
    Cups, 134
Dark Chocolate Pudding, 157
Easy No-Churn Vanilla Ice
    Cream, 166
Frozen Fudge Pops, 179
Frozen Raspberry Hot
    Chocolate, 185
Frozen Strawberry Cheesecake
    Pops, 178
Ginger-Lemon Ice Cream
    Cake, 182
Graham Cracker Lime Icebox
    Cake, 84
Grilled Peach Sundaes with
    Bourbon Caramel Sauce,
    167–168
Hot Fudge Brownie Sundaes with
    Spiced Candied Pecans, 169–170
Lemon Curd Tarts, 109
Lemon White Chocolate
    Truffles, 132
Maple Pecan Tapioca Pudding, 156
Mixed Berry Summer
    Pudding, 163
No-Bake Chocolate Peanut Butter
    Bars, 51
No-Bake Key Lime Pie Cups, 105
No-Bake Tiramisu Cheesecakes,
    69–70
Orange Panna Cotta, 153
Pecan Brittle, 141
Piña Colada Ice Pops, 176
Pink Grapefruit Granita, 172
Rocky Road Fudge, 138
Strawberry Balsamic Sorbet, 170
Strawberry Champagne
    Granita, 173
Strawberry Mousse, 145
Very Berry Frozen Yogurt Ice
    Pops, 177
Vietnamese Iced Coffee Float, 174
Whipped Lemon Ricotta
    Mousse, 146
White Chocolate and Toasted
    Almond Fudge, 137
Nutella
    Chocolate-Hazelnut Filled Scones,
        122–123
    Chocolate-Hazelnut Mug Cakes, 79

Nuts
    Bourbon Pecan Pie, 97–98
    Caramel Apple Yogurt Parfaits, 155
    Classic Chocolate Truffles with
        Hazelnuts, 133
    Coconut Almond Chocolate Chunk
        Cookies, 31
    Coffee-Poached Pears with
        Caramel Syrup, 162
    Dark Chocolate Cherry Bark, 140
    Grilled Peach Sundaes with
        Bourbon Caramel Sauce,
        167–168
    Hot Fudge Brownie Sundaes
        with Spiced Candied Pecans,
        169–170
    Maple Pecan Tapioca Pudding, 156
    Mexican Wedding Cookies, 33–34
    Pecan Brittle, 141
    Red Velvet Layer Bars, 50
    Rocky Road Fudge, 138
    Toffee Pecan Sandies, 32
    White Chocolate and Toasted
        Almond Fudge, 137

**O**
Oats
    Brown Sugar Cinnamon Stuffed
        Apple Crisp, 115
    Pear and Coconut Crisp, 116
    Whole-Wheat Oatmeal Cookies
        with Dried Blueberries, 27
Oranges
    Chocolate-Orange Sorbet, 171
    Mimosa Cupcakes with
        Champagne-Orange Butter-
        cream, 66–67
    Mini Carrot Cakes, 75–76
    Orange Panna Cotta, 153

**P**
Pantry staples, 7–8
Parchment paper, 5
Pastries
    Chocolate-Hazelnut Filled Scones,
        122–123
    Cinnamon Sugar Monkey Bread,
        127–128
    Coffee and Cinnamon Rolls,
        124–125
    Easy Palmiers, 130
    Maple-Glazed Donuts, 126
    Strawberry Shortcakes, 129
Pastry brushes, 5
Pastry cutters, 5
Pastry dough, 17–18
Peaches

Bourbon Peach Cobbler, 118
Grilled Peach Sundaes with
    Bourbon Caramel Sauce,
    167–168
Peach Hand Pies, 101–102
Peanut butter
    Flourless Peanut Butter
        Cookies, 26
    No-Bake Chocolate Peanut Butter
        Bars, 51
    Peanut Butter Banana Cakes, 81
Pears
    Cinnamon Pear Galettes, 106
    Coffee-Poached Pears with
        Caramel Syrup, 162
    Pear and Coconut Crisp, 116
Pecans
    Bourbon Pecan Pie, 97–98
    Caramel Apple Yogurt Parfaits, 155
    Grilled Peach Sundaes with
        Bourbon Caramel Sauce,
        167–168
    Hot Fudge Brownie Sundaes with
        Spiced Candied Pecans, 169–170
    Maple Pecan Tapioca Pudding, 156
    Pecan Brittle, 141
    Red Velvet Layer Bars, 50
    Toffee Pecan Sandies, 32
Peppermint Chocolate Bark, 139
Pie dishes, 4
Pies. *See also* Tarts
    Banana Cream Mini Pies, 92–93
    Bourbon Pecan Pie, 97–98
    dough techniques, 17–18
    Lattice-Topped Mini Blueberry
        Pies, 88–89
    Lemon Meringue Mini Pies, 94–95
    No-Bake Key Lime Pie Cups, 105
    Peach Hand Pies, 101–102
    Pumpkin Mini Pies, 96
    Sour Cream Apple Mini Pies,
        90–91
    storing, 9
    Strawberry and Dark Chocolate
        Hand Pies, 103–104
Pie weights, 5
Piña Colada Ice Pops, 176
Pineapple and pineapple juice
    Mini Pineapple Upside-Down
        Cakes, 74
    Piña Colada Ice Pops, 176
Pink Grapefruit Granita, 172
Puddings. *See also* Bread puddings
    Banana and Butterscotch Pudding
        Parfaits, 154
    Coconut Rice Pudding with Fresh
        Mangos, 151

Dark Chocolate Pudding, 157
Maple Pecan Tapioca Pudding, 156
Pumpkin purée
    Mini Pumpkin Cheesecakes, 68
    Pumpkin Flan, 159–160
    Pumpkin Mini Pies, 96

**Q**
Quick
    Caramel Apple Yogurt Parfaits, 155
    Chocolate-Covered Strawberry
        Cheesecake Bites, 131
    Chocolate-Hazelnut Mug
        Cakes, 79
    Chocolate Soufflés, 147–148
    Cinnamon Sugar Monkey Bread,
        127–128
    Classic Vanilla Cupcakes with
        Buttercream, 54–55
    Coconut Almond Chocolate Chunk
        Cookies, 31
    Coconut Cupcakes with Coconut
        Buttercream, 60–61
    Coffee-Poached Pears with
        Caramel Syrup, 162
    Dark Chocolate Almond Butter
        Cups, 134
    Dark Chocolate Cherry
        Tartlet, 114
    Double Chocolate Cookies, 29
    Flourless Peanut Butter
        Cookies, 26
    Frozen Raspberry Hot
        Chocolate, 185
    Grilled Peach Sundaes with
        Bourbon Caramel Sauce,
        167–168
    Hot Fudge Brownie Sundaes with
        Spiced Candied Pecans, 169–170
    Mimosa Cupcakes with
        Champagne-Orange Butter-
        cream, 66–67
    Molten Lava Cakes, 78
    No-Bake Chocolate Peanut Butter
        Bars, 51
    Peanut Butter Banana Cakes, 81
    Pear and Coconut Crisp, 116
    Red Velvet Mug Cakes, 80
    Spicy Ginger Cookies, 28
    Strawberry Clafoutis, 161
    Toffee Pecan Sandies, 32
    Very Best Chocolate Chip Cookies,
        The, 24–25
    Whole-Wheat Oatmeal Cookies
        with Dried Blueberries, 27

## R

Ramekins, 5
Raspberry Jam–Filled Mini Tartlets, 110–111
Red Velvet Layer Bars, 50
Red Velvet Mug Cakes, 80
Rhubarb
    Strawberry Rhubarb Crumble, 119
Rice
    Coconut Rice Pudding with Fresh Mangos, 151
Ricotta cheese
    Whipped Lemon Ricotta Mousse, 146
Rocky Road Fudge, 138
Rolling pins, 5

## S

Salted Caramel Cupcakes, 62–63
Salted Caramel Pots de Crème, 158
Saucepans, 5
Shopping, 6–7
Sieves, 5
Skillets, 5
S'mores Cakes, 82–83
Sorbets
    Chocolate-Orange Sorbet, 171
    Strawberry Balsamic Sorbet, 170
Sour cream
    Coffee and Cinnamon Rolls, 124–125
    Coffee Crumb Cake, 71–72
    Easy Palmiers, 130
    Fig, Honey, and Blue Cheese Galettes, 107–108
    Lemon Curd Tarts, 109
    Mixed Berry and Pastry Cream Tartlet, 112–113
    Sour Cream Apple Mini Pies, 90–91
Spatulas, rubber, 5
Spiced Chai Cupcakes, 64–65
Spicy Ginger Cookies, 28
Stay-at-Home S'mores, 135–136
Storage
    desserts, 9–10
    ingredients, 6–7
Strawberries
    Strawberry and Dark Chocolate Hand Pies, 103–104
    Strawberry Balsamic Sorbet, 170
    Strawberry Champagne Granita, 173
    Strawberry Clafoutis, 161
    Strawberry Mousse, 145
    Strawberry Rhubarb Crumble, 119
    Strawberry Shortcakes, 129

## T

Tapioca
    Maple Pecan Tapioca Pudding, 156
Tarts. *See also* Galettes
    Dark Chocolate Cherry Tartlet, 114
    Lemon Curd Tarts, 109
    Mixed Berry and Pastry Cream Tartlet, 112–113
    Raspberry Jam–Filled Mini Tartlets, 110–111
    storing, 9
Toffee Pecan Sandies, 32

## V

Vanilla wafers
    No-Bake Tiramisu Cheesecakes, 69–70
Very Berry Frozen Yogurt Ice Pops, 177
Very Best Chocolate Chip Cookies, The, 24–25
Vietnamese Iced Coffee Float, 174

## W

Walnuts
    Rocky Road Fudge, 138
Whipped Lemon Ricotta Mousse, 146
Whisks, 5
White chocolate
    Lemon White Chocolate Truffles, 132
    Peppermint Chocolate Bark, 139
    White Chocolate and Toasted Almond Fudge, 137
    White Chocolate Butter Cookies, 35
Whole-Wheat Oatmeal Cookies with Dried Blueberries, 27
Wire racks, 5

## Y

Yogurt
    Caramel Apple Yogurt Parfaits, 155
    Frozen Strawberry Cheesecake Pops, 178
    Very Berry Frozen Yogurt Ice Pops, 177

# About the Author

**Robin Donovan** is a food writer, recipe developer, and author of numerous cookbooks including the best-selling *Campfire Cuisine, The Deceptively Easy Dessert Cookbook,* and *The Baking Cookbook for Teens.* She lives in Berkeley, California, and blogs about easy recipes for people who love food at www.AllWaysDelicious.com.

CPSIA information can be obtained
at www.ICGtesting.com
Printed in the USA
BVHW020427120719
553174BV00006B/3/P